The Journey Home

Previous publications
All This And Heaven Too – A Study in Past Lives (The Greater World Christian Spiritualist Association 1996)
A Textbook of Healing (Prometheus Press 2004)

The Journey Home

Carol Brierly

Prometheus Press

Published 2005 by
Prometheus Press
c/o The Poetry Business
The Studio
Byram Arcade
Westgate
Huddersfield HD1 1ND

Copyright © Carol Brierly 2005
All Rights Reserved

ISBN 1-869961-96-X

Carol Brierly hereby asserts her moral right to be identified as the author of this book.

British Library Cataloguing-in-Publication Data
A catalogue record for this book is available from the British Library.

Printed by Antony Rowe Limited, Chippenham

Front cover photograph: 'Pembrokeshire Sunset' by Barry Stevens (www.mandalas.co.uk)

CONTENTS

	Foreword	7
	Preface	9
	Maggie and Mahel	15
1.	In The Beginning	17
2.	The Dimensions of the Earth	23
3.	The Second Dimension of Form	32
4.	The Third Dimension	39
5.	Moving into the Fourth Dimension	43
6.	The Higher Dimensions	46
7.	Angels	54
8.	The Predators	56
9.	Ascension	61
10.	The Hierarchies of Heaven	64
11.	Chakras – The Energy Centres of the Body	70
12.	Energies Which Influence Life Expression	75
13.	Sound	88
14.	Light	101
15.	Colour and Body Structure	111
16.	Validation of the Self	115
17.	On Oneness	124
18.	Love, Love Alters Everything	137
19.	Practise Random Kindness And Senseless Acts Of Beauty	146
20.	Living In The Fast Lane	152
	Daily Help	158

Foreword

Carol Brierly is an Aeolian harp. The wind of the spirit blows through the strings of her mind and the verbal music it plays uplifts and inspires. The strings are Carol's knowledge, professional training, experience of life and accumulated wisdom. In the words of the Gayatri the wind is that wind which pervades the entire universe, from which all things proceed and to whom all things return again.

The head will calculate the pitch of the strings, how exactly they have tuned and to what mode, and the exact notation of the melody and the harmonies. The heart will simply listen to the music and be moved by the beauty.

Max Payne
The Scientific and Medical Network

Preface

Mahel speaks:

Why is this book needed?

Life on earth at present for humanity is more demanding than it has ever been. There is a great shift of consciousness taking place. This change in consciousness means that people are being introduced to ideas and values that have never before been suggested to humanity as a whole, rather have they been the prerogative of those who have specialised in their focus, working in tightly remote groups. Now such phrases as, 'awakening', 'enlightenment' and 'conscious expansion' are being bandied about; indeed it is very difficult to avoid hearing them and many people are puzzled as to the real meaning. Many of the barriers that have formed the boundaries of human life and of human belief systems are now being taken down. Until recently people have lived within an isolated cell of consciousness, believing that they were the only form of consciousness upon this planet, not recognising that they are part of a much larger picture both on a planetary and universal level; but now in popular literature we hear talk of extraterrestials, of the Higher Self, of multidimensional energies and for many people this may appear confusing.

What do they mean?

One of the boundaries that is breaking down is that of conscious perception which monitors only that which can be received by the lower senses. By the lower senses we mean those of sight, touch, taste, smell and hearing. There are many forms of life that exist on a vibrational level that is out of the range of most limited human senses. The new awareness that is entering humanity is a connection with these higher vibrational forms of consciousness. One might call these forms lightbeings, extraterrestials, the higher self, spirit, God, whatever we will, but these descriptive terms simply encompass points of consciousness which inhabit a form which moves at a faster vibrational rate than the human senses of sight, hearing, taste, smell and touch can at present atune to. Within humanity a new sense has awakened: that of intuition. Intuition is a sense of faster vibrating levels of consciousness and it is able to tap into what we call multidimensional forms of life. These multidimensional forms are those that do not fall within the limits and boundaries of our present world. One has to move beyond old belief patterns in order to be able to move into the new paradigm, the new way things are.

In the last century, humanity has made great strides forward. Until that time, for example, a person who moved from one town to another would be considered a stranger, foreign, different. Within the last hundred years, we have begun to be a global community and it is not now unusual to see many different races and creeds all within the same environment, mixing and communing together. The next step for humanity is now to become more universally aware and to embrace the concept that not only are there global racial differences but there are also interplanetary differences and by this I mean other forms of consciousness, other ways of expression. You can call them extraterrestials. There are also those who at present do not inhabit what we would call a physical body, rather do they inhabit what we might call a body of light. These too are also forms of consciousness. They are just different, rather as an Englishman is different from an African; an African is different from a member of the Chinese community, the Chinese from the Asian, and so on. We are now expanding your culture.

In order to understand some of the basic new thoughts that will embrace your coming World, this book has been compiled. It is not the be-all and end-all. It is not everything that there is to be said about the subject, rather it is a beginning. It has been put together in order to stimulate your thoughts and ideas, because latent within you is a knowledge that is older and wiser than you realise and as you read the words in this book you will become open to a wider and more universal view of life. You will recognise that many of your belief systems are outdated, not because they were not of value but because they have outlived their usefulness. They were a stepping stone and it is important now to embrace a new understanding in order to be able to take the risk to move on to the next stepping stone of understanding.

The thoughts that are put forward in this book are not meant to be digested wholesale. Rather take from it what you are able to do at this moment and discard the rest until you are ready for new thoughts. If you have picked the book up and read it and feel, 'Well I know all that. I am way beyond these written words', ask yourself the question, 'Then why have I been drawn to read it?' Maybe you know these concepts but are you living them? Do you include them in your everyday expression or manifest what you know, or do you use it as a comfort zone rather than a creative zone for your new life?

I do not ask you to accept anything that does not feel right for you. There may be parts of the text where you think, 'No, I don't agree with that. No, that does not go far enough', or, 'that is inaccurate'. I ask you to take only that which seems right to your senses, which feels intuitively right for you. The rest, again, set aside. Recognise that each part of the text will have value for some people but not for all; it is not designed to be all-fulfilling, but is designed to stimulate certain aspects within certain people.

And who have been the authors? In your reality, Carol has been the author of this book. She has been helped by Maggie. In our reality this book has been authorised by many different beings who at this time do not inhabit a physical body as you would know physical bodies. Our bodies move at a much faster vibration than yours, faster even than the speed of light. Those of you with eyes to see may see us as Light Beings, but indeed our true consciousness is beyond the speed of light. Many of you know of our energies and will feel at home with us, Brothers and Sisters of Consciousness as you truly are. Names that you may recognise are: Serapis Bey, Khuthumi, Sananda, Sanat Kamura and myself, Mahel. We are all representatives of what could be called the Golden Ray. Representatives also of the Silver Ray, the

Angelic Kingdom are the Archangel Michael, the Archangel Jophiel and Gabriel. Mary also has helped many times with this text, and Athena. So already by picking up this book, you are picking up the energies of a multi-dimensional race, you are entering in to your multidimensional selves, you are embracing the concept, even if only subconsciously, of true multidimensional living and focus.

Having met us here we hope that you will meet us in many texts, in many ways and in many forms, because we can talk to you directly. We do not seek to impose our will upon Earth; we seek to assist the consciousness of humanity to move into a new paradigm, a new belief system, a new area of self-expression. We are here to help, for we ourselves have passed through this process in previous eras; we have experienced it many times in many ways.

We are not here as superior beings; we are here as brethren for we recognise you as brothers and sisters in consciousness. We also recognise you as those who are working valiantly to raise consciousness upon our planet Earth. You are our expressions upon this Planet and we honour and validate you. May the light shine within you and may your consciousness grow in joy and understanding.

We wish you well. Ayesha!

Maggie and Mahel

I am Maggie Lewis. I have lived in the North of England for most of this lifetime but I have a passionate interest in other cultures and therefore I have travelled extensively. I have known since very early in this lifetime that my purpose was to be a messenger for Mahel and I have been active in this way for about thirty years. Under Mahel's guidance I have also developed my own personality expression; hence I trained and worked as a teacher, and later I trained further in many complementary therapies, and with Esoteric Schools. Born in 1945, I have worked with Mahel in many ways and in many roles over huge cycles of time. At various times and always with Mahel's presence, protection and permission I have channelled other very beautiful energies that have included many of the Ascended Masters and The Christ. I love my life and my work, and those I am fortunate to journey with. Like everyone, despite Mahel, there has been times of upheaval, turmoil and crisis which only in hindsight have I recognised as the gifts they were.

I have always found it very difficult to describe Mahel in terms of 'who is he' because Mahel himself has always said he just IS. However over time, and having become used to being asked this question, he explained that he was a Cosmic Teacher. His specific purpose is to help humanity undergo the tremendous transition demanded by the dimensional shift currently taking place in this sector of the universe. This coincides with the entering into a new period of illumination sometimes referred to as The Coming of the Golden Age. Mahel refers to this New Age, when he talks to me, in terms of a changeover of energies. That is from the development in humanity of the ability to focus single-mindedly upon an ideal, objective or vision, to the incoming energy which heralds the predominant higher soul energies. This shift allows us to remember, redevelop and express our higher senses and faculties with less emphasis on the physical. The power of thought will then become the creative force within us.

His task is to help to prepare humanity by assisting them to develop their awareness in a variety of ways, by making them more conscious of the changes that are occurring within and around them and by being an energy they can turn to when they need advice and help with things that are directly related to these changes. He is a Cosmic Master having as he says 'ascended' the more localised energies and thus works freely in all dimensions and multiverses. He has no gender but at this time with this task uses the masculine energy because his task is to actively put forward energy to a receptive state (that receptive state being us). Receptively he links to the feminine expression. Thus he acts within the wholeness of the One and for the furtherance of the light of Divine Consciousness. Mahel rarely uses these sorts of complex terms when he is teaching; he prefers to put things in their simplest possible form. I have always found him a very gentle and loving teacher. I cannot remember a time when he has not been my constant companion in this life's journey.

1
In The Beginning

Carol takes up the story:

Hold on to your seats for this is Magic – MAGIC!

Not magic as we know it, but the high, high magic of the SPIRIT.

I'm not sure I can handle it, but – I'll try!

When this book was born, I asked Mahel, 'How did it all begin, is there a beginning and is there an end?' He laughed. He said, 'I will tell you the beginning at the end. You wouldn't understand it now.' And so I have had to wait until now and hope that some understanding has come through to me.

There was a reason for my question. I suppose really that I am a flat earther. I like to know when I reach the end of the universe that there is something to stop me falling off. And if there is not, what lies beyond. All rather childlike.

And now the difficult part. We were talking about past civilizations and why they died out, or apparently so. We spoke about the levels of consciousness of the peoples who were then on Earth. I find that I used the term consciousness wrongly, because there was a pause. And then Mahel said:

'Civilizations may end because civilization is an experience, but consciousness does not end. It is eternal, always part of Universal Intelligence. You are consciousness choosing the experience of Carol and the experience of the twentieth and twenty first centuries. But when that civilization ends, when the experience of Carol ends, your consciousness does not end. Your consciousness then chooses what experience it would like to embrace which, in the light of all others, would be most beneficial. So consciousness simply keeps being added to. It is continually adding to itself through all of these experiences. There is never a question of waste, single lives are never wasted, because that would suggest that an error had been made. There is no concept in multidimensional energy of error, other than the fact that many of you have had experience of life in a dual world and can therefore understand because you have had that experience. There is no such thing as a mistake because you have chosen literally every experience. There are no victims on Planet Earth, no victims universally anywhere. Everything that happens is a conscious choice which when seen from a greater perspective has enormous value. A life in poverty, a life of riches, a life of illness, is not wasted. Illness, for example, is the most profound teacher. There are many who choose to incarnate especially in the third-dimensional environment that you have on Earth for whom the illnesses that you would call serious are viewed from the spiritual, from the multidimensional level, as a privilege. They are an acceleration of experience, an acceleration of growth. They are expansive. They give acceleration of growth which would take thousands of lifetimes to get, and yet through one crucial serious illness you can experience levels of intensity, levels of understanding and being which are not possible in any other way. In the third dimension you do not always see things that way. So often from a lower dimensional viewpoint, this is judged from the point of view of a victim, as something that has happened to you over which you have no control. Looked at from this angle, you miss the purpose of the opportunity and the challenge.

'Third dimensional experience is valuable beyond measure. But only for a period. One wouldn't want to go on with one period for ever and ever, because that would rule out other areas of expansion, other areas of growth. Those of you who have completed a cycle in the third dimension must now bring in a different balance, a different perspective, no less precious and no less valid, but different.'

He paused:

'What lies beyond it all? I paused here because what lies behind it all is evolving consciousness, is the energy that we call God, the energy that we term Universal Intelligence, which is an ever-growing field of energy, all knowing, it is everything and yet on being everything, in being all-knowing, it 'lacks experience'. Therefore, everything that is known, everything that is, it seeks to experience, and as it experiences it becomes even more knowing, it adds to itself. This is the energy that we call God, that we call Universal Intelligence, this oneness, this wholeness, which is always an expanding field of reality, having no limits, no boundaries, only those that it seeks to impose upon itself in order to experience itself more fully. I am often asked, 'Is this energy then limited to the universe – is it limited to a galaxy, a solar system, a planet?' No, it is not limited to any of these, all these are but expressions of this energy and the only truth that has ever been said is that the Macrocosm is a reflection of the Microcosm and the Microcosm is a reflection of the Macrocosm, because energy can only reflect itself. Therefore this energy can reflect itself as a solar system in which each planet in the solar system is likened to an organ within a body and the space and currents that interplay in the solar system are rather like the circulatory system and the nervous system. This is the same within the universe. If you take a universe, then the galaxies and the solar systems become the circulatory and the nervous system. And you can say, 'What about the planet then?' and for the planet you have the various levels of space within the planet which you would call the sky and which you would call the earth itself, the ground, the vegetation that is there upon it. The different characteristics of that planet then become the organs, the circulatory system, the nervous system, and if you would look at any particular member of it such as a tree or an animal, you would find that each of these has its own particular characteristic. Even a single cell has its own nucleus, has the semblance of organs in different forms, the nervous system in a different form. Everything is just a reflection of that larger energy because that is what consciousness perceives itself to be. On whatever scale you choose to look at it, it clusters itself in these same sort of living forms, so that you can have the apparent organs, you have the same sorts of specialised forms of energy. It makes no difference whether you are looking at a universe, a galaxy, a solar system, a planet, or a specific kingdom, everything evolves around the same universal laws.

'That is the beginning and that is the ending.

'The most difficult thing to explain is that there is no beginning and no end, because energy always reflects itself. You may be consciousness inhabiting a human body, but you have the characteristics and qualities that are similar to an energy that in fact is inhabiting a planetary body or a galactic body or a universal body.

'There is no beginning and no ending, there is only the experience and as part of you is currently experiencing a human body, a part of that very same energy is experiencing an animal body, a vegetable body, a mineral body, a star body, a galactic body and a universal body.

'You have experiences in all these different forms. Where the consciousness is focused there are apparent separations, apparent boundaries and limitations. These, sometimes called 'ring pass nots', are fields of energy that you put about you in order to ensure that you perceive the experience you are wanting to perceive. If these boundaries were not there you would not know yourself to be human or you would not know yourself as animal, or as a planetary or solar body.

'So this is the explanation, so very simple, yet so hard to understand. What you are is what you will be, only the form changes, the vibratory rate of energy, yes, that changes also.

'When you step off the edge of the body, then you enter that which is like a nucleus of energy. This has been called many names. Some people call it the Self, or the Higher Self, the Monadic Energy, the Essential Essence, the I AM. Yes, it has many names but it is the nucleus of your energy, the awareness of what is going on in the dimensions. And from that nucleus you will decide when you wish to extend your consciousness next. It is as if you have withdrawn your consciousness into its nucleus so that you may consider the next move. There are many different choices. You may decide to reappear in incarnation upon earth to complete a cycle of incarnations. Or you may have already completed the cycle and thoroughly experienced human form. On returning to the Essential Essence the question may be, 'What form is now going to be my next adventure?' A number of options will be available to you, but it may be decided that it is not quite time to take on a universal body. Perhaps the step from a humanoid to a universal body is too expansive. On the other hand, a universal body might now be the very best, because it is so different from the humanoid experience. All of these things become available to us and the choice is ours.'

2
THE DIMENSIONS OF THE EARTH

There is a great need at this time for the human family to be able to see itself more clearly in a wider context. In order to be able to do this we need to expand our understanding and relationship with the space in which we live and with its natural laws. It is hoped that this book will help those who are awakening their higher senses and greeting a new era of being, one which will bring understanding of their true nature as energy manifesting through form, with the emphasis being placed upon the former rather than the latter. When we concentrate so much on form which we often refer to as 'physical structure' or body, we limit ourselves to the world of effects rather than understanding the world of causes which lie within the outer bodies – the energy bodies of all that is energy made manifest. When we move into these energy realms two great influences not as yet fully understood or appreciated by man, have great relevance. These are *sound* and *colour*; both will be discussed in greater detail in later chapters.

Sound within the multi-universes is the creator of all form. So in our ancient teachings we have been told: *'In the beginning was the Word and the Word was with God and the word was God'.*

Many have pondered this statement; few have understood its significance. The word that was uttered was not 'God' – that is how the original text has been translated. This reference is symbolic. The 'word' that was uttered was of significance because of its sound signature, its harmonic resonance. It was not in the true sense a word but rather a collection of sounds, like a mantra. Those sounds, when projected, set in motion specific energy movements that scientists may describe as chemical reactions or mathematicians as formulae, but which in esoteric terms is known as the act of creation. The sound of creation is not the sound that lies within the frequency of the normal human ear. The sound of creation is of such a high vibrational value or nature that it is beyond the frequency range of dense form, thus the human body though responsive to these frequencies is not able to hear them.

Sound on higher levels of vibrational frequency is not auditory in nature but could be likened to pure focused precise thought. This as it vibrates to a lower frequency expresses what we describe as sound, though is very much more than our current understanding of the phenomenon.

We can however begin to understand the power of sound as a creative, as well as a destructive, force when we remember that the high notes of the human voice can shatter glass. And that sound can produce many patterns and forms that we can see in the natural world around us. Sound can create or destroy.

Sound is the pure potential of creation and can be likened to the energy that is the basis of the most advanced pure mathematics. It is present beyond the reasoned understanding of even our most advanced physicists, though certain breakthroughs are imminent. It gives rise to the science of geometric forms on all levels of vibration, and creates oscillations of energy that take wave form at lower frequencies and which carry the blue print energy in its most creative potential, carrying the intelligence of the desired creation. On the planes or dimensions, which vibrate at higher frequencies, sound is the creator of universal DNA, indeed upon the nature and balance of every cell within the human body. This is also true of these structures within the other life forms. This will become an area of intense scientific and medical interest, and of major importance to us all.

The higher sound has frequencies and fluidity, an almost wave-like structure, its frequencies being very specific according to the type of energy or sound being manifested. It can be varied with great precision depending on the desired result. In the realms of lower frequencies of vibrational dimensions, it is a very tangible energy and one that we experience for ourselves, varying in pitch, volume and tonal quality. Thus sound at this level (the lower realms mirroring the higher) can be attractive, constructive, repellent or destructive; indeed it can be anything, for as has been said, it is the energy of the creative process.

All the planets have within them a specific note. The Earth is part of a grid. The note spreads out like a wave to form a pathway of energy which is a very complex highway of intelligence. Where there are nodal points within the pathways this is where form as we would call it is created. The planets therefore all have their specific spatial web that connects them within the greater web, because when a sound is specifically created the first thing that happens is that it creates a web which is made up of geometric forms and forces, smaller wave bands which act within the range of the original. The forms most closely connected with the Earth for instance are those of the triangle, the diamond and the dodecahedron: these are the characteristic symbols of the Earth and although they have geometric characteristics, they also have a resonance which is found in all molecular and submolecular states. The laws which govern these particular resonances also govern any larger forms created by their larger masses. Every planet has its own geometric forms and resonances specific to its own velocity, and specific to its own network of light. It is this that predetermines the type of evolution that can take place within that energy.

Man is at the point of a great breakthrough in many fields that will greatly expand understanding of the energy worlds which surround us and this in turn will change the way in which we live and interact with everything that is. For aeons of time humanity has been exploring the physical outer world, and always emphasis has been placed upon the physical – with the exception of a few highly developed pockets of consciousness manifesting in smaller human groups where the emphasis was more esoteric, and where the development of the energy fields took precedence. Hence the legends around such groups in the times of Lemuria and Atlantis, and the more recent influence of Tibet. It is becoming obvious, even to the most dedicated explorer of the physical, that the answers to the many imbalances being experienced at this level do not have their causal effects there.

One of the first principles of the creative force of sound is that it has the ability to create specific frequencies, zones of energy. These have been referred to in many esoteric texts as planes or dimensions of consciousness. Each dimension is a sound frequency within specific range parameters, which produces a vibrational frequency coloured by its own laws of energy. These laws of energy, which are often called by esotericists 'Divine Laws', are precise in mathematical terms. Therefore each dimension of vibration is able to express consciousness in its own unique way according to its own laws of manifestation. These dimensions of consciousness are becoming more accessible to human awareness and many previous barriers caused by the limitation of the human mind and perception are about to be removed or are in the process of being so.

Form is created through the manifestation of sound – the first by-product of which is light. It might be said that light and therefore colour is the first act of creation. Light contains all colours. Colour is sound taking form. The light so produced forms a grid or network of light energy along which consciousness can travel. The light network is rather like a highway for sound and consciousness. Sound frequencies are played – as light (and therefore colour) along the grid, causing it to oscillate in a manner which becomes even more attractive, so increasing its light frequencies, and these cause a gathering of intelligent energies at pulse points and focal points – the various aspects of form as we know it.

On Earth the first dimension of form expresses itself through both the more volatile elements – the gases, the many liquid energies – and those we would *consider* as being most solid – the mineral element. All of these forms have consciousness, they are not inert states, and they interact according to the laws of that dimension and vibrational frequency. These are the areas of physics, chemistry and mathematics. They in turn have developed into further fields of specialisation. What we are just beginning to understand is that as human consciousness seeks to penetrate these other forms of consciousness, both are changed irrevocably. They start to interact and interrelate on levels previously not experienced on Earth by either form.

Every level on the first dimension – the gaseous, the crystalline or dense matrix – is a different expression representing a different state of the vibrational nature of this dimension. The viscous element has an upgraded form, which expresses as crystalline. Each expression similarly can be said to be a progression of the other. A very simple analogy could be taken by considering the element of water. Water when heated becomes vaporised, the vibrational rate of the molecules rises and we see it as steam. Conversely when the steam is cooled, i.e. when the vibrational rate is lowered, it returns to its original liquid form though in some instances a more purified version, some of the impurities having been driven off. Lower the vibrational rate still further by cooling and ice, a solid, is formed. This is a very simple analogy but no one who has seen the molten rocks spewing from the lip of a volcano can fail to recognise a parallel. Rock in turn when heated can become fluid, and when cooled returns to its solid state, but it may change its expression, e.g. by the formation of a crystalline or gem-like structure or by becoming more radio-active.

Intelligent consciousness flows through all these states, and all have their own specific plan and evolutionary goal. Within the mineral kingdom in the state often described as 'solid' there is a most definite progression of conscious evolution – that of mineral – crystal– gem to radioactive substance. Whilst the first kingdom like all others is in a constant state of change – it forms the basic structure on which all other material forms can grow, live and have their being within given limits. A concept which may not be new to some people is the fact is that this first dimension has an intelligent life force energy or consciousness. As man breaks through the limitations of the lower senses and taps into senses more in tune with the energy bodies surrounding the physical body, then communication between the levels of consciousness will become increasingly possible.

It is time to be aware that those things we consider most solid are in fact not so. They appear solid but are in fact particles in constant motion. This motion is of a slower vibration than the human sensory system is unable to perceive. When viewed through a high-power lens, it is found that in even those material objects considered most dense, the spaces in between the particles appear huge, indeed they look like outer space with the planets appearing at intervals.

The intelligent nature of all material form is in fact a sub-kingdom of that form and comes under the umbrella form of a life force called the Devic Kingdom. It is this intelligent life force which is responsible for the evolution, care and maintenance of that form.

The Earth shows an amazing diversity of form within this first dimension. It has therefore a wide range of Devic activity and influence. Remember *all* form comes under the jurisdiction of the Devic world – this includes the human body! The consciousness which dwells there is self-perpetuating and has its specific and group agendas.

The first dimension of our world is the *planetary body* we

call Earth. Earth is then a living consciousness, a 'being in its own right experiencing a planetary body' – just as we are a consciousness in our own right experiencing a human body! The Earth then is a 'body' with its own 'skeletal, muscular, circulatory and nervous systems'. Of course we do not refer to them as such. To us they are the heavy gases, the molten and solid states, and we can also include the gases which surround our planet: oxygen, carbon dioxide, nitrogen and the small quantities of rarer gases and the vast expanse of water surrounding the land masses. Each part has its own specific characteristics and functions within the whole. The Earth then is a body – just as our physical frame is our body. The first dimension is the densest form and base energy from which all else manifests in the *material* worlds.

The care of the Earth is the responsibility of a differing type of consciousness from that of our own, one which has a very much faster vibrational rate that renders it almost invisible to the human senses. The task of the Devic Kingdom is to ensure free flow of energy around and through the form; this includes the energy bodies which surround that form. In all cases, with the exception of the human, there is a close relationship and co-operation between the form and its devic caretakers and the consciousness within. Humanity has currently divorced itself from this relationship, and therefore the physical body is becoming less robust. And because humans do not recognise the need for this symbiotic role, they also ignore it in the other kingdoms of nature. Thus our planet is suffering imbalance with all the consequences we know so well. This severing is often referred to as a man being separated from his soul. Earth is not the norm within our solar systems. The diversity shown upon our planet is a unique phenomenon. On other planets in our system, there is a more selective and narrow field of development and experience, and this is reflected in the second, third and fourth dimensions of life.

3
The Second Dimension of Form

The second dimension arises out of the first dimension of form. This second dimension could be described as a hive of activity and is of particular diversity, colour and range. It is closely interwoven with its own Devic Kingdom, the world of the fairy, whose task is to ensure the energy balance and well being of this level of consciousness. So close is this relationship that it appears almost symbiotic in nature.

The Devas, or fairies, working within this area are in themselves a world within a world. They manifest an extreme diversity of form much as does the Human Kingdom when we consider the various races each portraying different characteristics and producing vastly different cultures. The Devas work within the plant world. In the past, this kingdom, the Devic, was visible and accessible to many humans. However, as the human kingdom evolved towards its industrial and technological eras, so the Devic families receded from their sight. As humans lost touch with their own interdependency with the natural kingdoms and with their own intrinsic essence, their ability to interact with the natural energies diminished. This is a cyclic phenomenon and not as many view it a catastrophic degeneration of humankind. A pathway was chosen which determined human and devic experience for an era of time. It then became necessary for the two to work separately and man chose to look outward and explore the world outside himself. Man is now choosing to turn his attention inwards and once again to enter the world of energy. It will be found in the coming years that as people become more and more aware of the Devic Kingdom, they realise and understand their purpose and activity and once again work in harmony and co-operation with them. For the Devic Kingdom, the path of expression is one of total service. Each plant, each form within the vegetable kingdom has its caretaker, each group of plants or species has its own type of devic expression working with it. Many of the differing types have been held sacred within our myths, legends and fairy tales. The latter are the stories, contacts and interactions of old times, passed down from generation through generation, to ensure that the thread of contact would never be totally lost. And, so that they might be remembered, the Devic Kingdom has kept contact with many small children within the human kingdom, whilst they are still aware of their energy bodies. Fairies, elves, gnomes, goblins – these are nations within the Devic Kingdom. Each has its area of interest and expertise. Each has its own affinity with natural flora and fauna, and each comes in contact with the other, much as the human kingdom has its national and international connections.

So often we in human form refuse to believe what we cannot see. The Devic Kingdom is accessible to us but it is we who must adjust our vision and awareness.

Imagination is the residual pathway of communication between our physical and our energy bodies. It is a sense within us, which is directly related to our energy patterns outside of incarnated form. It is an energy language and pathway of communication. There is nothing that man has created on Earth which hasn't been received in the imagination first. Imagination is our basic creative energy; it is our first language; it is an expression of universal energy, which is totally neutral. It is neither good nor bad. It simply *is*. Thus imagination produces information which is pure essence. Good or bad has relativity to the environment and culture within which it finds itself. Through imagination we are able to access all that is, universal consciousness in its most essential essence.

As we come to accept the form being shown to us in our 'mind's eye' and to hear the voice of the Deva in our inner ear, then we may find that as we look at our plant or natural friend, on it or close to us we will physically see a wispy mist, which eventually will appear to differentiate into a form – a form we may well associate with tales told from our fairy stories. Be still and keep your movements, thoughts and feelings at whisper level. Just allow yourself to *'be'* present as an observer, and allow the Deva to direct what happens thereafter. From this point we may well find that we are able to make direct contact and communicate with the Deva of our chosen second kingdom expression, and go on to meet many others. We must remember that their preferred communication will always be telepathic because of the differences in our vibrational rates.

The more the human kingdom awakes to its own inner world, the more accessible will become the world of the

Devic Kingdom.

Each individual within the human kingdom also has its own devic caretaker – once again it has 'kept faith' through our stories, myths and legends and this caretaker we refer to as our 'Guardian Angel'.

Annie Besant was a member of the Theosophical Society which was founded in the late eighteenth century by Madame Petrova Blavatsky and Colonel H S Olcott. The declared aim of the society was 'to collect and diffuse knowledge of the laws which govern the universe'. This aim was revealed in Blavatsky's two great books *Isis Unveiled* and *The Secret Doctrine*. Among the early members was Thomas Edison, the inventor of the electric light bulb, and Charles Leadbeater.

On the death of Madame Blavatsky in 1891, Annie Besant became the head of the Theosophical Society and with Leadbeater began to investigate and record their observations and investigations into the higher levels of consciousness and conditions after death. Many of the books are now out of print but can be found in the libraries of the Theosophical Society. In contradistinction to some of the other books produced by the Society they are clearly expressed and make for interesting reading.

Charles Leadbeater as well as being a visionary was a highly developed clairvoyant and in full possession of higher vision. He could see quite clearly the nature spirits, the devic forces appearing on the astral plane and described them in detail.

Enter now Geoffrey Hodson who seems to have had even more developed etheric and astral vision. This had been with him since childhood. At first he saw nature spirits inadvertently in the way that a small child sees them, accepting them as part of the natural background. Living in the north of England, in Preston, he had access to the countryside and spent much of his time watching and describing what he saw in the fields and gardens and in the house itself. In his books, he gives vivid descriptions of the nature and habits of the English spirits and fairies, dividing and subdividing them into different types, describing their movements and habits and determining their function in the natural world. Both Leadbeater and Hodson used their higher sight in other lines of investigation, perhaps in some ways more fascinating than their investigation of nature spirits. They were able to describe the structure and inner make-up of atoms and chemical elements. Hodson's clairvoyance in particular enabled him to see at subatomic level. He could see inside an electron. Besant and Leadbeater found that there were 'ultimate physical particles' beyond which the atomic particles disappeared entirely from their sight. Eighty years later these UPAs have now been postulated by physicists. They have not yet been seen. But two early theosophists actually saw these smallest indivisible constituents of matter and investigated their different numbers and arrangements in the different chemical atoms.

These worlds have now been explored by people who have been able to develop their acute energy senses and allow them free expression. The findings are only now being scientifically honoured as far as the various chemical components are concerned. Their accuracy is profoundly significant. They also documented the nature of the Devic Kingdom in relationship to the first and second dimensions. One breakthrough preceded the other.

As man moves forward in a conscious expression of the multi-dimensional world, so he will become the uniting force. There is a great move into this arena, but although described as sub-molecular and genetic research, it is not recognised in its true significance.

Peter Tomkins and Christopher Bird in their book *Secrets of the Soil*, quoting from Alexis Carrel, write, 'Plants are great intermediaries by which the elements of rocks, converted by micro-organisms into humus, can be made available to animals and man built in flesh, blood and bones. Chemical fertilisers can neither add to the human content of the soil, nor replace it. They destroy the physical properties and therefore its life. Plants that are chemically fertilised may look lush, but lush produces watery tissues which become more susceptible to disease, and protein quality suffers.'

It would seem that all the non-infectious diseases that have developed over the last two centuries can be related to the environmental toxins produced by our industrial society and our lack of understanding of the role which the Devic Kingdom plays in maintaining the integrity of plant energy. So often man believes that the Nature Kingdom is insensate, it has no feelings. Again there is here a lack of communication of proven fact within our societies. Scientific research has proved that without doubt plants can 'see'; not as we see but they are able to move towards or away from light. They can communicate with one another, particularly plants within the same species group. Recent experiments in the United States have shown that the 'cry' of one plant can be heard by another. Plants can count; they can recognise friend and foe. They react to touch. Have you ever touched a mimosa leaf? They can open at sunrise, at the exact time the sun is rising over the horizon, even though the sun is obscured by cloud and it is still quite dark. In Russia experiments have shown that plants have a nervous system which responds to all the wide and varying emotions that animals and humans have, and in much the same way.

Consciousness is not the prerogative of any one kingdom. It is a universal phenomenon. It flows throughout each dimension and operates through all form associated with each dimension. Only the expression of consciousness differs, communicating in ways which we are only just beginning to understand.

4
THE THIRD DIMENSION

Within this dimension, we have the expressions that have developed mobility. The emphasis here is towards the development of collective or group consciousness. All the animal forms are included and it also includes the human form. Indeed human consciousness, until such time as it becomes self-observing and self-recognising as to its inter-relationship with all other forms of consciousness and divinity, is developing within the third dimension awareness.

The third dimension is very much focused upon material existence in relationship to the outer world. Group and tribal focus is very much a theme, with the group, herd or tribe providing a safety net for all members, and it is a means of increasing the odds on survival. Group initiation increases inter-dependency one upon the other. It is a basic formula for survival and community living. It ensures a greater degree of security in what may seem like a hostile world. Each tribe or group has its own rules, behavioural code and hierarchy, irrespective of whether the collective consciousness is animal or human.

There are three main development arenas within third dimensional living. The first is the rule of the group or tribe in order to survive. Secondly when survival is no longer an issue, the feeling-nature begins to develop as desire and greater selectivity – survival is no longer the main consideration because it is assured to a greater or lesser degree; now there is concern for the quality of survival. Thirdly, the development of the thinking-nature is developed which leads to a form of individuation, a standing out in the crowd – leadership through planned action rather than the rule of might. The reproductive process here requires an individuation and separation into masculine and feminine expressions, both of which are highly defined. In the third dimension much emphasis is placed upon the mating ritual and rearing and survival of the young life tends to revolve around these. All effort is directly or indirectly related to these two central themes.

We have been taught that Homo Sapiens, the human form, has evolved from animal forms. This is definitely not the case. The Animal Kingdom and the Human Kingdom are energetically differing species with totally differing paths of evolution. They share some characteristics within the third dimension – indeed more than most humans would like to admit! But they are widely different in other ways. Until now, animals have been able to express a role, which is purely service. The path of development within the strictly animal kingdom (excluding Homo Sapiens) has been that of wild animal to domesticated herd to domesticated pet. In the last leap, the animal changes allegiance from its own natural group to affiliation with the human tribe. The animal kingdom is often thought to refer to those animals which have not developed the upright spine or which are four legged, or which are not able to manipulate their environment. These forms are also most often seen as being a lower form of evolution. This is not so. They are a different type of form, and they have a very different vibrational rate and sensory range to that of Homo Sapiens. They are here to develop specific energy characteristics, which to some extent overlap those of man, but are not identical. Whilst humans seek to dominate and change the environment as part of the challenge to develop the Will, the animal kingdom works in harmony with the natural world and learns its place within it. For animals, the third dimension is not an arena for developing creator consciousness, but rather one for developing co-operation. For humans the third dimensional work is an introduction to the creation of the Will and to the ability to impose that Will.

This is an important difference to note. Third dimensional man is truly not much interested in co-operation. The emphasis is much more on imposing a collective Will upon the environment. This has given rise to territorial patterns of behaviour with the need for defensive energy. Successful communities give rise to nations which hold domination over huge tracts of land.

Within the third dimension animals also attempt to mark their territory and defend it, but sooner or later they are forced to accept the more dominant energy or force – the human Will. Co-operation is a path of learning for animals – just as the development of the Will and creativity is a learning path for humanity.

The laws of third dimension are very much based upon duality. The boundaries are highly defined. Codes of ethics and living are precise and enforced. Power tends to be manipulative and aggressive. As consciousness rises and begins to reach for a higher manifestation of expression, then it can appear that chaos and anarchy rule. The rigid tribal laws are challenged. Life no longer stays in the neat categories laid down by the hierarchical system.

5
MOVING INTO THE FOURTH DIMENSION

Our world is now moving into the fourth dimension. Until now there has appeared to be a separateness of consciousness within the lower dimensions, each one having its own specific purpose and agenda, pursuing this in what seems to be almost isolation.

But now with the move into the fourth dimension, the various kingdoms are becoming much more aware of each other – they seek to communicate, to interact and co-operate. Each dimension, first, second and third, seems to be opening up, sharing its secrets, no longer following its own path independently of others, no longer working for itself alone. All forms of consciousness seem to be moving towards wholeness, towards integration of consciousness.

To those of us who love the natural world the change is evident: plants, animals and birds are starting to communicate with us, the rocks beneath us, particularly the crystalline forms are sharing their secrets. No-one who has studied crystals can doubt this. Is this because we ourselves are becoming more open and seeing what we have missed before? Partly perhaps, but not entirely so, the shift in consciousness is a reality.

This is of major concern at the present time upon Earth because the Earth energy itself has now adjusted to the fourth dimension and a great wave of humanity is now being swept into fourth dimensional awareness. Man is now dividing into two major species with increasingly less in common. Within the third dimension there remain those who still have the need to experience third dimensional awareness before they can move on. They will gradually die out on Earth and find other areas where they can fulfil their reincarnation and expression. Those who are moving forward within fourth dimensional experience will remain upon Earth. Their higher senses will develop their intuition first and then clairaudience, clairsentience and clairvoyance. In fourth dimensional man the consciousness changes from group consciousness to individuated consciousness which works in co-operation with others. It is at this point that we will all become aware of the Devic worlds and this will lead to increasing communication and understanding. This also gives greater insight into the energy fields around us and of higher vibrational forms existing in other dimensions. We will no longer be bounded by space and time because we will live and move within these areas.

As these changes begin to take place within fourth dimensional human consciousness, the animals are also changing. They open to a wider range of communication and expression and all kingdoms of nature will begin to show fourth dimensional characteristics. Many of us can see this beginning to happen now; we see changes of behaviour patterns particularly in animals and birds which have become domesticated. Communication is often by thought rather than sound and care for each other becomes the norm. The change has begun. The life as we knew it begins to fade to distant memory. This shift of consciousness is not an overnight phenomenon. It tends to happen in a cyclic pattern, periods of awakening alternating with times of assimilation.

The fourth dimension is like a bridge. It links the lower dimensions of form to the higher dimensions of expression. The fifth dimension enables us to focus the mind and thought and allows the development of the higher mind, which is able to work with multidimensional energies. These are the dimensions of form beyond which physical form as we know it does not exist.

In the sixth dimension we are not fully in form. We begin to see where we are going and we co-operate in the venture. Our emotional nature changes. We now know where we are going and what we must do to get there.

Beyond form there lies the area of pure consciousness. In the seventh dimension there is no form as we can recognise it. Thought is now a creative force and gives rise to understanding, from which comes the desire to create the vision, the result of which becomes form as we know it.

6
THE HIGHER DIMENSIONS

The fourth dimension is based on concepts of time and space. Gradually the ability develops of being able to move into moments that are timeless. This comes through the practice of meditation and sometimes through the spontaneous experience of the individual where they are lifted out of the limitations of the third dimension and moved beyond into the space/time frequency. They come into a state of pure being. This is one of the levels where the consciousness of people may reside upon when they die. It is a level that is not nearly as physical as the one that they have left.

When people die they may enter into any plane of consciousness, depending upon their level of evolution and upon the level of experience and evolution that they have reached at that particular time. Cycles of incarnation and learning are such that one rarely leaves behind the realms of matter too distantly.

The fourth dimension has been compared many times with the Astral Plane which is purely a realm of illusion, of feelings and emotions. Many people believe that the Astral

Plane is real but it is only this belief that gives it apparent reality. After death these convictions many ensure that they enter the Astral Plane, but sooner or later they are able to free themselves from it by recognising the illusion. It ceases then to exist for them.

The fourth dimension is also a realm of feeling, but of higher feeling where we begin to create through those desires, which because of strong feeling relate to strong vision. We are here in a realm of creative activity, and creative activity is the great builder. If the person has reached a slightly higher degree of understanding then the consciousness may dwell in the fifth, sixth or seventh dimensions awaiting another opportunity to continue their cycle of learning. The seventh dimension is very often where you will find those who are engaged in what we call rescue work, the enlightening of consciousness of those who have passed over but dwell on the illusory fourth dimensional level. These beings work then to bring more light into their understanding, to broaden and widen so that they can recognise that the prison that they are in is of their own making.

Those beings of higher vibrational resonance who wish to work with the consciousnesses that are now experiencing earth and are working to advance the higher vibrations of the Earth, tend to base themselves on the seventh dimension. The seventh dimension is rather an interim base, for those beings. If one is wishing to work with the Earth plane, it becomes very necessary to have experience of the seventh dimension, because one is then able to downstep the vibration so that it is tangible from the lower vibrations, the third in particular.

Beyond the seventh dimension our senses are not able

to pick up higher vibrations because the frequency would be pitched too high. All the dimensions occupy the same space and time. Time is something which is merely used as a measuring tool but a very convenient one. In spatial relationships there is really no difference other than the frequency of the vibration. When we talk of multidimensions they exist in different frequencies of the same spatial arena. Of course the spatial arena is much larger than we are aware of, for as yet we have not had the capacity in our third dimensional consciousness of experiencing the universe. Scientists know that beyond the solar system there are thousands of galaxies but no one knows truly the boundaries of the universe. There will be a time when we will talk of the multiverses as commonly as we now talk about the universe. Nevertheless the dimensions that exist within space and time exist within us and there is no barrier to stop people coming in or out of dimensions. The only barrier is the person's own capacity to raise their vibrations.

There are those beings who are able to move up and down the scale at will and there are others that have accepted the limitations of the dimension and are therefore at this time not able to do this. This is what the Earth is experiencing, the whole issue of the transition that the Earth is going through. The Earth itself has been undergoing a third dimensional experience and is now moving to a fourth dimensional experience. Humanity upon Earth has been experiencing limitation because until now the Earth has been a third dimensional planet; the third dimension has its own ceiling, its own limits; it cannot see further until a certain point has been reached and then it can increase its speed of vibration and as it does this it raises itself nearer and nearer to the next degree of consciousness. This is what is happening with the Earth. The Earth has enabled itself to pass into the fourth dimension and now everything that is within the boundaries of the Earth has the capacity of moving into a higher range of frequencies. Instead of having to build everything with their hands or mechanically. as has always been the case, people are now able to listen to their feelings and connect with their knowing and also with their vision. Once we pass beyond the third dimension into the fourth, there is an almost automatic access into the fifth and sixth dimension. The feeling is given by the knowing which is propelled by the vision and all of these interplay with each other. People have moved beyond the dimensional limitations and have moved into the realms of their intuition. We will find also that some people will have had fourth, fifth and sixth and to some extent seventh dimensional experiences. These will be no surprise to them. When we are at this level we will be able to say that when you absolutely know something that it isn't a belief any longer. It is something that every shred of your being knows. Psychometry is on that level. People pick up something they 'know'. They can feel the energy when they hold it and this is when they 'know' the whole pattern of its past. Psychometry is an example of a fifth dimensional attribute. Many experience the sixth dimension, one of future enlightenment. There are those times when you can be talking to someone or listening, or you could be meditating and you lose all sense of time, all the sense of your body, of feeling, all sense of thought. Then you come to, and three, maybe four hours will have passed in what feels to be the twinkling of an eye. This is a seventh dimensional experience. Everything is intermingled once the third dimension has been passed.

Everyone is moving inwards, not upwards as we tend to think, on what is like a vortex into the Essential Essence which is beyond space/time frequency, beyond form; and it feels as if one is in a whirlpool. They are going back to God. And as they go back to God, it is as if they are being pulled inwards to the core of their very energy centre. It is like a lightening. Each time you are pulled into a different vibration towards the centre you are moving faster, which is what it actually is doing because the vibrational frequency that it is working with is a faster moving frequency. There are still those on earth, still those in our own communities, who are living life at a much slower pace. They are still living in the third dimension. Their understanding is at a lower level, it is moving more slowly.

As we move beyond form it is like entering the very centre of a hurricane where there is absolute stillness. You find that there are various states within that stillness. These are beyond our capacity to understand, as yet.

Previously when people were going to move through different levels of consciousness they would move out of the body to do so and they would move into lighter and lighter bodies, i.e. they would then incarnate into the fourth dimension and would have a lighter body. It would still be a body but it would be less dense, and then perhaps they would choose to incarnate in the fifth dimension of awareness and they would have a lighter body still, until by the sixth or seventh dimension, it is a light body that shimmers but nothing that you could touch. What is happening now is that this transformation is taking place without the need for people to leave their physical body. The physical body is going through an evolutionary process. The physical body itself is being upgraded. It is undergoing change and that change is a biological change. Change is taking place with the cells themselves, within cellular consciousness which because it is changing so is cellular structure. The body is changing though the endocrine system which in itself is undergoing change, and therefore the chemical stimuli of the body is changing. The electrical circuits of the body are changing and as a result the nervous system is changing. The circulatory system is changing.

All of this is why at the present time people are experiencing so much difficulty with aches and pains, with vertigo and with many symptoms which in truth are because of the upgrading of their body from one dimension to the next.

There are many things for which scientists and doctors can give no explanation: why people have so many allergies, so many viruses. Viruses belong to fourth dimensional consciousness, they are not three dimensional. This is why science has such difficulty tracking viruses because the science of today is third dimensional. Scientists can get a glimmer of understanding but cannot understand their form, because they have no form. As science moves further into understanding of viruses so they move further into fourth dimensional things and as they start to do this they will start developing the tools so that they can look into the fourth dimension. It is an upgrading of consciousness.

There are now scientists who know that human anatomy and physiology are changing. Cellular structure is changing. It is changing at the levels that are beyond quantum physics. Science is getting to the point where it knows that energy itself knows itself and can be whatever it chooses to be. This is fourth dimensional and they are now looking at the cells within the physical body. The consciousness of the whole of the physical body is undergoing change and this can be measured scientifically. We know that change is there. The twelve strand DNA is a point in question and is coming to the point of logical conclusion. The information has not as yet been released to the general public because it is not yet acceptable.

There are more questions than answers at the moment and further findings create only further questions because there is no scientific basis for this knowledge. For understanding, there has to be a total redefinition in order to understand what is happening. There are people who have already made the leap in understanding and so the knowledge is available to them. The next three to five years are going to be vital for the understanding of consciousness on Earth. There will be tremendous changes. Already people know that change is taking place in their physical bodies. Moving through our limitations is uncomfortable but this discomfort will pass … sometimes it is because we are thinking that we have not the knowledge. The reasons that we have viral problems are because we are between dimensions. Viruses are the natural consciousness of the fourth dimension. When we are totally fourth dimensional there will be no disharmony between our vibrations and the viral vibrations. At this present time the fourth dimensional virus is being used to accelerate people's growth and when people undergo viral infection, there is little that medical science can do to help them. We have to enter into fourth and fifth dimensional understanding in order to come into harmony with the virus. This is why some people with the AIDS virus may go into complete remission because they suddenly have a vision of sixth dimensional quality of how they can change their lives in order to rid themselves of this problem. If you lift out of a level, you lift out of the illnesses connected with that level and this is what is happening to the viral illnesses at this time. They are very much fourth dimensional.

Anything which is in a dimension is within people in that dimension. (The macrocosm is within the microcosm and is the microcosm.)

7
Angels

The Angel energy does not incarnate into physical bodies. It is a fast moving energy which has no form. It can sometimes project an illusionary form like a thought form but this can only be seen if we can raise our higher senses above the third dimensional level. Unless we are able to do this we cannot see angels.

It is the task of the Angelic realm, or the Devic realm as it is sometimes called, to maintain the energy of our subtle bodies when we are incarnate. Each one of us has what we call a Guardian Angel, one that is totally responsible for maintaining our subtle bodies: sustaining the subtle body energy and the physical body energy, just as the devic energies maintain the energies of the plants and animals in the lower dimensions.

When we become aware of our higher dimensions moving into the higher levels of the self, then these higher levels bring to us all the experiences necessary for us to become spiritually strong. Sometimes it feels as though all Hell has been let loose for the Ego resists the change. It may feel that we die to be reborn. We are changing our energy field and our physical body in having to adapt to this. At times we feel spaced out and uncomfortable for the body finds it difficult to cope with the higher dimensional frequencies which are now part of our lives. Life as we have known it goes into upheaval. Why is this?

The task of the Angels is to bring us what we need, not what we want from the level of our Ego. It is to separate us from the Ego in order that the higher energies can take control. The Ego does not like this.

How do we know when separation from the Ego has occurred; when the higher energy is in control? We can find the change within ourselves. The Ego is self-centred, full of likes and dislikes, of mood-swings and fears. The higher energy is calm, it is knowing and it is unafraid. It feels like being in the eye of the storm, where all things are quiet and still.

The Ego has served us well in the past. It has enabled us to grow in many ways and to experience many things which would have been impossible without it, but as it becomes stronger it tends to lose contact or to feel separation from the higher spiritual energies. It is at this point that separation is necessary; it is here that we are ready to move on. We may look back and see many things we do not like in ourselves; experiences where we still feel shame and guilt, but they are now becoming past and our future is very different. We do not know what may lie ahead but we are ready to meet the challenge. We shall not fail.

8
THE PREDATORS

Let's have a little light relief and I will tell you about the Predators, often called the Fallen Angels, although they were not truly angels as we know them but a higher group of beings who came down to experience and develop through life on earth. When the Earth was first formed, it was as you may imagine exceedingly hot. No life could exist in that heat. It took many millions of years before the Earth cooled and only then did the first unicellular organisms appear. Were they plant or were they animal? We do not know. For a long time nothing else happened. Much of the Earth was covered with water, slowly receding to form the great oceans. Even then the Earth was not known as we know it now. The north and south poles lay on the equator and the land would have been to us unrecognisable. Among the earlier land masses was Gondwanaland situated in the area of our South Pole. Later a vast mass called Lemuria filled the Southern Hemisphere and this in turn sank giving rise to a smaller island mass in what is now the North Atlantic Ocean. We know this as Atlantis.

57 THE PREDATORS

Earth has been used as an experimental area for dimensional growth. Within this area, plants, animals and man have been 'seeded' from other stars and have been allowed to develop according to their nature. Development completed, many of the species have withdrawn, their future development being continued elsewhere. Evidence of their previous existence can be seen in what has been left behind, usually skeletal imprints and bones. Man was not one of these early species and did not appear until later. He too was seeded; the suggestion is that he came from the star, Sirius.

The first generation of beings other than animals to live on Planet Earth were more multidimensional than ourselves. Their task was purely as caretakers of the Earth. They were known as the Brotherhood of Light. They had all the information for the development of life on the planet and development of the planet itself. Sound was used for creation and a knowledge of the mathematics of the energy of sound was a pre-requisite. About this time a group of these higher beings seized control of the Earth. Known to us as the Fallen Angels or the Predators, they believed that they had the knowledge and ability of the Creator – which they had not yet acquired. Not so – the correct encoding for creation and source energies were not there. They did untold damage to the communication systems and to the race of man which had now settled upon the Earth. They were responsible for a great deal of genetic engineering and cloned a race of men as slaves destroying the higher energy centres of their victims. Those who were prepared to work with them in Atlantis were spared and were allowed to retain their genetic capabilities as long as these did not override those of the Predators, otherwise they were disabled and became little more than lower animals and were used as beasts of burden.

Both the Predators and those of the Brotherhood who had remained faithful were present in Atlantis, the Predators occupying the central low-lying areas and the south of the island and the higher group of Beings in the mountainous north. Here much of their work in their halls and temples was concerned with the healing powers of fractionated light-colour, by passing the light of the sun through massive crystals onto the affected patient.

Atlantis sank and those of its peoples who were not drowned or who had left earlier were scattered throughout the northern world, to the now emerging islands of Ireland and the British Isles, westward to the areas of South and Central America, penetrating as far as Peru, and eastwards to the Mediterranean areas, North Africa and Egypt. Little remains of the island-continent of Atlantis other than the small group of volcanic islands off the west coast of Africa which we know as the Azores.

And the Predators?

The Predators are still with us as I know to my cost, but their power is diminishing. They are unwilling to recognise this and their intention is to do the greatest harm in the time remaining to them. This is monitored and controlled as much as possible. But the Predators have firm control of a few people in key places. The Earth is ruled by six groups who recognise one energy. This one energy is not a Lord of Light and the six rulers are not the obvious people. They appear in this way because this is how they work. It is important to recognise that the six are in communication with the One. This being is a Predator but not in incarnation on Earth. It is a stellar base on one of the outlying planets of the Pleiadian System. Whereas, in general, the Pleiadian System is a part of the Intergalactic Federation we must recognise that not all Pleiadian life forms are part of the Federation. The Predators have control of some of the planets of that system.

The present position is that once again our planet and this sector of the galaxy are returning to the Light. Those who are actively working for the Light on this planet – the Lightworkers – are the energies of the original creators who have incarnated throughout this cycle of the Predators and who allow the higher energies to work through them in the interests of the planet and its peoples. Many of the people who work amongst us are Lightworkers who are acting as encoders. They send out energy which unlocks and decodes other information.

When we look at the world around us it may not always seem so. It can seem as if progress is barred for some of us and limitations are removed for others. We see suffering and pain around us and apparent success through evil deeds. We must remember that everyone has choice and many of those who are at present incarnate have chosen to experience the lives that they lead, some for the physical limitation which can include severe illness or deprivation and others through allegiance to powerful and negative energies basking in their perceived power. So it is important to choose wisely. This Earth will enter the fifth dimension and those who choose to remain with third dimensional limits may do so. The only difference is that they will live in a different dimension. Nothing will change for them. Nothing will be lost. They will merely evolve at a slower rate. There is no question of being set aside or cast out. They are not yet ready to move forwards into the multidimensions but every intelligence must move at its own rate and cannot be forced. The beauty of this is that many of the perpetrators of the troubles on this planet now recognise that their way was not the right way and they too have come into the Light. So everything has been gained, nothing has been lost. Moreover the energies of those who have never had to live under the two-strand DNA structure have gained a wealth of information and knowledge and they now act as advisers to the High Council.

9
ASCENSION

We hear a great deal about ascension these days. Ascension has to be understood as a transmutation of consciousness, as a step forward. All previous barriers, limitations and narrow perceptions are removed and a new frequency of vibration is allowed to introduce form. Ascension on Earth affects the various levels of consciousness in different ways. For humanity, ascension means the conscious recognition of responsibility for the self and for the self as a representative of the whole. The ascension that we talk of now means that the consciousness becomes aware of intelligence and energy beyond previous limitations that have been part of Earth development and we start to see the Earth and ourselves as part of a much larger whole. Initially the connection will be seen within the solar system, and then there will be a shift which will embrace the intergalactic networks, the consciousness moves to that of being galactically aware and then the universe will appear as if it were almost as close as part of our world.

Ascension is the widening of the net of understanding,

the embracing of all forms within the universe. The previous ideas about the ascension, for example the leaving of this earth in the form of a dove, arose because of the genetic engineering which has been carried out earlier on humans. Ascension was seen as a leaving of the body behind. We know now that this is not so. The myth also became linked with the visits and departures of extra-terrestrials in spaceships. Limited humanity evolved its own myths.

Many of us still believe that in order to ascend, to go into a more evolved state of being, the physical body must be left behind. The creation of this belief was a way of manipulating humanity until such time as the genetic encoding had been altered. This was the first example of genetic engineering and was carried out by the group of energies that we know as Predators. The human being had originally twelve energy centres, each centre being a direct line of communication to a higher Being, a Lord of Light and able to receive information from that source. The majority of the centres were closed down and the energy centres that were necessary to life only were left. These were the base centre, the sacral and part of the solar plexus. A partial energy was left in the solar plexus but it was a very mutilated section. When this happened, man lost connection with all but his form and the product of that form. Humanity lost touch with the consciousness of the planet and of other planets and became animal in nature. Man could no longer contact the higher beings of the planet. This is the time in Atlantis when the twelve strand DNA was severed, leaving only two and a half strands. It broke the connection and the pathways of consciousness.

It is not the divine plan for Earth either to be invaded or evacuated. Earth has been under the influence of free will energies who have been able to exercise part of their evolution on this planet. The Predators also were in the process of evolution and Earth came for a time under their control. All consciousness as it evolves has a tendency towards arrogance and the Predators were no exception. They attempted to control not only the Earth but also humanity.

Nothing has been truly lost by the action of the Predators. The total growth and awakening of humanity has been postponed but the ability of the Lords of Light and of humanity itself has been strengthened and it has given the opportunity for consciousness to incarnate upon the planet in a direct way and this has become a very informative process. So nothing has been lost. Those who were Predators are to a large degree leaving the planet and have moved to a much greater understanding. Some of them have remained; they find it hard to let go but many of these are now very willing helpers in the process of reawakening humanity for they now realise that their own process of growth is tied to the evolution of humanity. Until they release humanity they cannot pass to the higher levels and the test for them lies in being able to reconnect what has been disconnected. As yet they have not evolved sufficiently to be able to work from the awakened centres.

10
THE HIERARCHIES OF HEAVEN

When we talk about the hierarchical system we become involved with the multiverses and then I get really out of my depth. So let us limit ourselves to the universe as known on Earth, remembering that other universes exist and these also are headed by a cohesive universal energy. This energy is an intelligence and could be described as being an individuated intelligence, although it is not individuated in the way that we would understand with our third dimensional minds. It is an intelligence that expresses in a unique individual way but is still part of a much larger whole. The head of our universe is known as the Father of Time, or The One that Is. It is part of a central intelligence around which are gathered the heads of other universes.

When any new Light Energy such as our universe is to be evolved and formed, representatives from these other spatial areas are chosen to accept responsibility for the task.

When the universe that we are part of was being formed, twenty-four beings of light were chosen to be a directive influence within that energy concept. They were known as the Council of Twenty-Four or The Lords of Light. They are the decision makers and have the whole picture, the vision. These energies have counterparts and they interweave to form two types of light which are known as the Gold and Silver Rays. From the Gold and Silver Rays comes all manifestation on the dimensional frequencies – the two energies blend and combine together in order to create the energies of form within this universe. All colours of light originate from interactions of these Rays. The Silver Ray produces the Angelic Realms and the Golden Ray the Elohim. The Angelic Realms are able to manifest the vision, i.e. a sort of blueprint; and the Elohim have the task of creating an energy from that vision which in turn will bring forth a form. That form may be a vapour. It may be an energy type, photon energy for example. It may be a material form such as we experience upon Earth. The Angelic Realm is creator of the vision, the Elohim brings the vision into being. We have descriptive terms for these energies. All that derives from the Silver Ray, the outer light is a creation of Metraton energies. That which is focused through the Elohim, through the Golden Ray is the Cosmic Christ. Together they create what is called a Ray Factor.

Universal energy recognised that in order to create specifically it needed to divide itself, and so did so, into seven major forces of creation. It began by dividing itself into the Trinity – the Trinity was the first Ray, the Ray of power, the Ray of the Will of God fed through universal consciousness. This became held by the First Ray and was termed the Master knower of creation. From the Ray One energy, two further energies were birthed. Ray Two became responsible for holding the vision and, like an architect, drew up a plan showing how what was wanted could be produced. Ray Three, the Ray of Intellect, was the builder and created the form. Help was needed in the production and other energies were created to enable this to happen. These are minor Rays of expression.

The Fourth Ray came into life expression to create beauty and harmony through art. It became known as the Ray of Harmony through Conflict, through the development of an ego which needed to give way to the higher self. It encompasses duality and through duality brings a whole harmony.

The Fifth Ray became the Ray of Science, the Ray which bridges the lower and higher mind. It brought new information into expression through active knowledge and intellect and is very specific.

The Sixth is idealistic. It holds the focus and brings higher thought through into practical expression. It is linked with geometrical form and with ceremony and ritual in order to bring about all that the other Rays have prepared the way for.

All these Rays work together in various cycles of expression in order to bring about the divine plan. Their influences can extend over a day, a month, a year or thousands of years as in the greater cycles.

Various cosmic minds or energies work with the Rays as part of their development. They are called the Lords of the

Rays. They do not always stay with the same Ray energies but move from one to another, building up different experiences. They are high spiritual energies who have at one time lived on Earth; lived a life of love and service to the highest and to their fellowman. They have now passed beyond incarnation and unless, as Mahel says, they 'borrow' a body, are rarely seen by us and then only if we are able to lift our consciousness as high as the fifth dimension.

Many of the higher energies or Masters are unknown to us. We are all returning to the higher levels of the spirit that we know as God and they are the forerunners who are guarding us on our way. Those masters influencing the Ray cycles have had lives as far back in time as Lemuria and Atlantis and many great and influential lives since then; interesting detail is given at the end of this chapter.

The various schools of initiation were always affiliated to one or other of the Rays. Some were affiliated to the Christ energy, the energy of the Second Ray, others to the energies of the First Ray.

The Seventh Ray is not bound to any particular school of thought. It brings in universal knowledge and comes through knowing. We do not need to fight for causes and beliefs. We must fight to make sure that we ourselves are peaceful and harmonious, allowing this to flow out to those around us. We must correct our own imbalances and start to use our higher senses in the service of ourselves and others. Life around us is undergoing great change.

Lords of the Rays

El Morya
Chief of Darjeeling

Lord of the First Ray   Blue Ray
Council of Great White Brotherhood.
Previous lives:
Abraham 2100 BC
Akbar – Mogul Emperor
Melohios – Wise man of Egypt. Birth of Jesus
Arthur – King of Britain
Thomas Becket
Thomas More
A Rajpal Prince of India – Mou Wong

Lord Lanto

Lord of the Second Ray   Yellow Ray
Previous lives:
High Priest at temple in Lemuria
Ruler in China in time of Confucius

Paul the Venetian

Lord of the Third Ray
Previous lives:
Veronese Artist 1528-88
Previously an Atlantean
Inca Ruler in Peru

Serapis Bey

Lord of the Fourth Ray
Previous lives:
High Priest in Atlantis
Went to Luxor before end of Atlantis
Leo Midas in Sparta
Amenhotep III – built temple at Luxor

Hilarion	Lord of the Fifth Ray Previous life: St Paul
Lady Master Nada	Lord of the Sixth Ray Previous lives: Priestess in Atlantis Lawyer – Justice
St Germain	Lord of the Seventh Ray Previous lives: High Priest in Atlantis Joseph – Father of Jesus (Alchemy) St Alban Head of Plato's Academy Merlin Roger Bacon 1214 Christopher Columbus – 1451-1506 Francis Bacon – 1561-1628 Returned as St Germain (French Revolution)

11
CHAKRAS – THE ENERGY CENTRES OF THE BODY

Long, long go, before time began: before man made time, for time is man-made, the human body had a twelve strand DNA. Each strand subserves one energy centre of our being and we must think of the centres in terms of the whole being and not just in the part that we can see, and feel and touch. We must understand also that all centres are not only interconnected but each subserves the others. Thus the throat centre as well as 'serving' the surrounding areas serves the heart, the emotions and the higher centres.

We have known for a long time that there are centres outside the physical body and it is now the time to consider these and integrate them into the whole

The seven main chakras are in the body, starting at the base of the spine and moving upward. We know of five more outside the body, making a total of twelve. Oxygenation, light and conscious intention will activate these centres, and once they are switched on, the challenge is to translate all of the data that is carried through them to the DNA strands.

The chakras inside the body can release our body memory,

our body experience from this lifetime, as well as from other incarnational journeys.

1st chakra Stores the core identity: it deals with who we are and how we survive. It allows us to journey into ourselves and the foundation of our core beliefs.

2nd chakra Relates to creativity and sexuality: it opens the record of our beliefs and experiences in these areas.

These first two chakras correspond with the traditional knowledge of the two strands of DNA. The issue affiliated with identity, survival, sexuality and creativity which have challenged us for millions of years.

3rd chakra Relates to the solar plexus and the gut. When open, it assists us to feel our way through life. In women, because of menstrual bleeding and childbirth, this area is often more active and is regarded with respect. The will, power and feelings lie there.

4th chakra Aligns with our heart and when open connects us to all life. Compassion flows from this centre, allowing us to understand the why and wherefore of what we perceive. The flow of compassion takes us beyond judgement, which acts as a trap to separate us.

5th chakra Is found in the throat, opening the great gift of vocal expression.

6th chakra Activates the third eye, stimulating the ability to see beyond the third dimension.

7th chakra Is at the crown of the head. When open it connects and circulates spiritual energies to the cranial area. Once stimulated, the pineal and pituitary glands, as well as the hypothalamus, play active roles in linking.

8th chakra Is in close proximity to the physical body – anywhere from a few inches to a few feet above the body.

It is symbolised by a Silver Lotus and is known as the Soul Star and Cosmic Gateway. It relates to the invisible realms outside the body.

9th chakra Is outside the Earth's atmosphere, perhaps as far away as the moon. We visualise it symbolically above the 8th chakra, as a four pointed pearlised gold star, known as the Planetary Gateway.

10th chakra Reaches into the Solar System, offering access to all that is. It is known as the Intergalactic Gateway and can be visualised above the 9th chakra as a mist of pearlised pale blue.

11th chakra Is a galactic chakra that offers information about local stellar influences. It is visualised above the 10th chakra as a cascade of pearlised rose pink light, and is known as the Christed level.

12th chakra Reaches outside the galaxy and gives access to what is in the rest of the universe as we picture it. It is visualised as a pearlescent light, and it is the Higher Self Activation, above which is seen the Merkabah Light Vehicle, a brilliant gold five pointed Star, which holds the blue, white and gold light bodies.

In general we do not have access to information outside our universe as we picture it, because our bodies are not sufficiently evolved to handle it.

These twelve centres must be accessed from inside, where we can feel the data corresponding with them and translate the experiences within the context of the mind. This is ourself, evolving into our multi-dimensional identity, remembering who our version of ourself is – out in the galaxy and beyond.

Many of us have been taught that we evolve through

reincarnation and that we have a soul that has many versions of itself. This is only a small part of the picture. We understand our re-incarnational selves are not all human. They exist in a variety of shapes, sizes and guises, showing that all is part of the one.

THE TWELVE CHAKRA ALIGNMENT

Holy Spirit

White Dove

I AM presence — Opal

Stellar Gateway	Peach
Soul Star	Gold
Gateway	Magenta
Causal	Aqua-blue
Crown	Violet
Brow	Indigo
Throat	Mid-blue
Thymus	Turquoise
Heart	Green/Pink
Solar Plexus	Yellow
Sacral	Orange
Base	Red

Earth Star

12
ENERGIES WHICH INFLUENCE LIFE EXPRESSION

by Maggie

These vital energies govern our lives and influence our character make up. We have a tendency to think of Universal Energy as God, or we give it titles such as The One Light, The Creator. If we take the concept of 'as above, so below', we can begin to understand that this creator energy has facets to its character or expression just as we do.

Universal Energy also has these same varieties of expression. We know of seven that are of major influence in this universe; each has a very specific role and function that manifest on every dimension of creation. These roles or functions have each formed a kind of structure within the dimensional arenas. Each of these structures are rather like political parties or business enterprises in that they have their own specific agendas and they each have their own members or 'workers'. And within each there is also a hierarchical system, earned not through lobbying, but being most fitted through achievement and experience for the roles they play and the sphere of influence they have. The members of each exist on many and various dimensions of being. These great organisations are non-competitive and non-manipulative, rather they serve specific functions for the good of the whole. Equally, we could say that the Universal Energy is rather like a huge university and each department represents one of the Rays. People come into contact with the Ray or department that has meaning for them at any given time. Seen in this way it can be understood that some people will deal with one or maybe two or three departments in their lifetime, others having little relevance to them. Our interaction with the Rays is much the same, individually, nationally, globally and on a larger scale – this also applies to solar systems and galaxies.

The Rays are universal, indeed multi-versal in their field of expression, but each corner of the dimensions needs only the attention of certain Rays at any one time.

Each Ray has a specific area of interest and focus, and has recognisable functions and qualities.

The important thing for us to understand is that these Rays affect our lives on all levels. They influence all life as we know it. They influence those things which we consider to be inert, which are in fact also expressions of energy, consciousness and being but are out of our dimensional, therefore predictable, range. They are energy differentiating into qualities of expression that hold within them specific focus and intent. Every expression of energy is experiencing its own evolution, therefore has specific needs in order to be able to develop most fully according to its present potential. Those expressions choosing similar experiences will be attracted together and they will be drawn to arenas which are influenced by the Rays of energy most beneficial to them at that given moment of their cycle of becoming.

The Ray energies are, or would appear to us to be, constant, though in truth they too are evolving. They do not manifest their full potency universally all the time. Rather, various parts of the universe experience a variety of the Rays most suitable for the environment of experience they offer. Our solar system for several cycles lasting several millions of years has been influenced by the seven Rays of manifesting energy. These Rays have varied in potency in their influence in order to allow evolution to flow in a predetermined manner. All seven in our solar system moderate their energy to work in harmony with the Ray under whose greater responsibility our solar system falls. This is the Second Ray – the Ray of Love and Wisdom. In order for these qualities to be developed most fully the other six Rays move in and out of influence as experience demands. Thus a change over of Ray energy is at this time in progress and we are moving from a period during which we have been encouraged to develop our individuality, passion and idealism to a new avenue of expression where we will be called upon to realise the potential of the power of thought as creator. For this to be possible we will be drawn to the need to recognise and stabilise our body, emotions and minds as tools for a more encompassing intelligence within us. As we develop the ability to focus with intent we will find within us the ability to create our world as we would wish it to be – not just with our own selfish desires in mind but in alignment with the good of the collective.

Let us look most closely at each of these Rays, considering them as departments of a large governing body. This government however is non-competitive and works from a plan that has been agreed by all.

The Ray energies will be looked at as qualities and attributes which are relevant to humanity – that being our arena, but recognising that the smaller is a reflection of the greater and vice versa we realise that these principals expand out into greater expressions of consciousness with more far reaching purpose than we are able to grasp at this moment.

Ray One is often known as the Ray or department of Death and Rebirth.

Its task is to ensure that systems break down when they have outlived their usefulness in order that new and more applicable orders can take their place. This Ray can often appear ruthless because it works with the larger picture, the less personal perspective. Its influence brings qualities of leadership and if not moderated by love this can manifest as dictatorship. It brings the ability to be decisive and incisive, clear in action, able to make decisions, which are wide ranging. The good of the individual must give way to the good of the whole. People influenced by this Ray are often innovators, people at the leading edge of society in whatever field of expression they have chosen. They will challenge the status quo. They carry the winds of change and theirs is not an invitation to take part, rather a decree of what will be. This Ray requires actions and acts with a strong will and determination. The colour associated with this energy is red and in many ways its nature can be considered as volcanic.

Negatively expressed it can be full of pride, wilfulness, arrogance, tyranny and a desire to control others, to make them subservient. At its best it can give balanced yet decisive leadership, strength, courage, truthfulness and fearlessness and the ability to grasp the larger view of things in a balanced and comprehensive manner.

It has often been said that First Ray people take the kingdom of heaven by storm. They knock on the door and insist upon an answer.

The *Second Ray* is known as the Ray of Love and Wisdom. It has also been called the Christ Consciousness

The energy of this Ray brings a thirst for knowledge and understanding that gives way to wisdom. This Ray encourages the development of the intellect. The ability to see oneself as an individual being. People under its influence love to learn – to study to gain knowledge, which they turn into a spiritual rule of living. It can bring intuition and wisdom.

People influenced by this Ray are able to become excellent teachers and diplomats. They are good at passing on to others a true view of things. Whatever their chosen field of expression they will most often teach through this – though they will not always recognise that they are in fact teaching, preferring to think of themselves as communicators. This Ray brings patience, endurance, a love of truth, calmness and strength, faithfulness, intuition and clear intelligence.

As with all things in this arena where duality is our greatest teacher, negatively expressed it can be much less pleasant. In this sector of the universe we are learning about the freedom of choice – with all that that implies. Its drawbacks can be over-absorption in study to the exclusion of others, coldness and hardness because of an over-development of the intellect not modified or balanced by the heart, which manifests as a total indifference. There can be contempt for the mental limitations perceived in others.

This Ray leads us to desire to explore our environment and to want to know more about it, to understand it.

The *Third Ray*, known as the Ray of Active Intelligence or the Higher Mind, is the Ray of the abstract thinker or philosopher. The first Ray, having destroyed old forms and created our new environment, and the second Ray, having led us to search for understanding and knowledge of this new order, allow the third Ray to philosophise about the possibilities. People under this influence are able to grasp the essence and wider view of things. They ponder deeply until they are led into the realms beyond those in which is the already obvious and known. These people often delight in higher mathematics. It is not enough to know that something is, they need to know why it is. They have the capacity for high degrees of concentration, the ability to understand abstract intangible ideas, a sincerity of purpose and patience.

Negatively expressed this can manifest in intellectual pride, coldness, inaccuracy in details, selfishness and being over critical of others.

The *Fourth Ray*, that of Harmony through Conflict, is a Ray and energy which teaches us much about duality, about polarities. People experiencing this Ray so often live lives of extremes. They are either very happy or totally down in the dumps. Their world is either fantastic or awful. The qualities of doing and being, passive and active are so equally proportioned that the person can become confused. Ray

Four people love ease and pleasure, they can let tomorrow take care of itself or they are all action, fiery and impatient feeling as if they are at war with themselves, their world and struggle is all they see. This results in rapid evolution. This is the Ray that influences humanity as a whole. It brings enthusiasm and a love of having plans and purpose. A love of colour and melody. The ability to quickly recover from adversity. People whose Ray this is as a major influence can be brilliant conversationalists but can be prone to gloomy silences and they can for a time feel overwhelmed by sorrow and perceived failure. They can be delightful, but difficult to live with. Other qualities are generosity, sympathy, strong affections and devotion, quickness of perception and physical courage.

Negative expressions lead to lack of moral courage, self-centredness, inaccuracy, extravagance and proneness to worry unnecessarily.

The *Fifth Ray* is known as the Ray of Concrete Knowledge of Mind.

This Ray allows evolution of the mind and advancement of an expression of energy along technological lines, giving the experience of yet another form of creativity, and one which has been of great influence within the human family. This energy brings the pursuits of scientific research and a keen intellect. Whilst it influences humanity as a whole, the individual with specific affinity with this Ray will spare no effort to verify every detail. He likes to penetrate matter to understand the underlying laws of nature. To see and understand the energy behind the manifested form. People under this influence are extremely truthful, have a great need to search for facts which they like to explain lucidly at great length – they can therefore be boring to others less passionate about their subject. Their path of life is through scientific research pushed to ultimate conclusions and accepting the inferences which follow. They are given to strictly accurate statements, justice, perseverance, common sense, independence and keen intellect.

If negatively based this may manifest as narrow mindedness, a highly critical nature, extreme prejudice and a lack of sympathy and reverence.

The *Sixth Ray*, that of Devotion and Idealism, is just withdrawing from our influence after being prevalent for a cycle of some two thousand years. We all therefore bear some of its qualities more or less. This Ray brings an appreciation of colour, beauty and all things lovely. It gives the ability to have strong opinions which can lead to being full of religious instinct and the need for a personal god. These people will lay down their life for an ideal – for what they believe in, but they will not necessarily lift a finger for someone who does not support their cause. They can be fanatical and tend to see things as either perfect or intolerable. People around them are seen as friends or foe according to whether they support the same cause or not.

By prayer and or meditation they move towards union with God – but they are prepared to fight and kill to get there in *their* way.

The strong attributes that come from this energy are love, tenderness, loyalty and reverence. Negatively expressed, however, this energy can show as selfishness, jealousy, prejudice and too rapid conclusions.

The Ray which is now becoming most prevalent for us is *Ray Seven* – The Ray of Ceremonial Magic and Order

This Ray requires that we learn to balance our personality expression – the body, emotions and mind, and learn to focus upon our inner wisdom. It awakens the higher senses within us, leading us to expansion of consciousness into higher dimensions of being. This energy likes to have all things done in an orderly fashion; therefore it encourages forethought, planning and attention to detail. It likes to do the right thing at the right moment. Balanced perspective is high on the agenda. It encourages self-responsibility – indeed personal responsibility is a great issue. It interprets responsibility as the *'ability to respond'* appropriately and according to the person's own choice in any given situation. It therefore encourages strength, perseverance, self-reliance, extreme care in details and courtesy.

When out of balance it can manifest as too formal and rigid imposition of laws, narrow and superficial judgement and over indulged self-opinion.

Because each human being represents a mini-universe within themselves they all are influenced by their own specific Ray pattern. This Ray pattern determines our character, our hopes and the dreams which drive us to manifest our potential and pursue our evolution along specific lines. The Rays affect all energy, therefore life anywhere. It is important to understand their impact in terms of Earth and more specifically humanity.

Whilst the Human Kingdom is influenced by and incorporates all seven Rays, those that predominantly influence the evolution of humans at this time are the Fourth Ray, Harmony through Conflict, and Ray Five, Science and Concrete Knowledge, which allow us to achieve knowledge through discriminating choice. Only in humanity are the three major Rays found in their full influence: Ray One (Will or Power), Ray Two (Love and Wisdom), Ray Three (Active Intelligence). Individualisation is now required to give way to group consciousness and this results in initiations and great personal transformation. Individuated or if you prefer 'self-conscious' human beings have now reached the stage where they are aware of the greater world in which they live, and they are becoming increasingly aware of extra-terrestrial life forms, which expands their arena of consciousness still further. Human beings evolve in stages of soul growth and there are humans representing every level.

Considering now the individual person rather than humanity as a group, we must realise that each human being is under the influence of a larger number of Rays – though not necessarily all seven. The totality of the Ray makeup gives the individuals specific energy type; we are each a complex and unique energy form.

Each one of us is influenced by:
- the solar Ray (Ray Two, Love Wisdom)
- the Planetary Ray of Earth (Ray Three, Active Intelligence)
- the Rays of Humanity as a whole (Ray Four, Harmony Through Conflict, and Ray Five, Science)
- the Ray of our own Soul which may be any one of the seven Rays

- the Ray of our personality which may be any one of the Seven Rays

The Human Kingdom is the only kingdom on earth through which all the Rays are expressed.

The Animal Kingdom is influenced by Ray Three (Active Intelligence or Adaptability). This Ray has a very strong influence leading the animal consciousness towards animal one-pointedness. When this point is reached Ray Six (Devotion and Idealism) cyclically urges the animal consciousness towards the goal, which is relationship with man. This can be seen in action through the domesticated and 'tame' animals, which live very much in harmony with man, and through those which have been domesticated but have not yet achieved a degree of harmony.

The Animal Kingdom is divided into three categories:
1. The higher and domesticated animals, such as cats, dogs, horses, elephants
2. The so-called wild animals – lions, tigers etc.
3. The mass of so-called lesser animals such as rodents

The Vegetable Kingdom is influenced by three Rays:
  Ray Two – Love and Wisdom
  Ray Three – Harmony through Conflict
  Ray Six – Devotion and Idealism

The Mineral Kingdom is influenced by:
  Ray One – Will and Power
  Ray Seven – Ceremonial Order

At this point Mahel stopped and said

'Well that's it, Carol. Now finish it yourself!'

And when I had recovered from the shock

I did!

Now read on …

13
SOUND

'In the beginning was the Word and the Word was with God and the Word was God'

'All things were made by Him and without Him was not anything made.'

Sound, the creator of form, the builder. Creator but also destroyer. We must never forget that sound can also destroy.

When the great stone circles were first built, the energies of sound were used to raise the stones. Not by man, he had not yet the ability to do this. When the Pyramids took form, sound again was the creator, in these and many other great buildings. There is a story in the Far East of the raising of a great wall. Massive stones ... too heavy to lift. The priests and their acolytes stood before the wall and behind the priests the people. After the appropriate rites had been performed, the High Priest raised his arm, and the people sang one single note. One clear note; and the stones, now light, were raised into place.

Many civilisations have passed and left no trace. Who knows how often sound has been used as builder and as creator. But the echoes remain. We are told that the World was formed by a single sound; the so-called Big Bang theory. Whether the theory is true or not, we have historic evidence of sound as a creator of form and equally so as destroyer.

We read of Joshua, the son of Nun and the servant of his God who walked with his people around the walls of Jericho for seven days and on the last day for seven times …

> and it came to pass at the seventh time when the priests blew on their trumpets before the Ark of the Lord, Joshua said to the people, 'Shout'. And when the people shouted with a great shout, the walls fell flat and the people entered the city and utterly destroyed it.

It would seem that Joshua himself wrote the description of that particular event. It filled nearly a chapter of the Jewish bible. We can be sure that he filled in the detail, and that he wrote it for future generations to read. The event made its mark and we still sing of the time in the Negro spiritual, when 'the walls came tumbling down.'

And we hear of the soprano singing a sudden top note and shattering the glass chandelier with the sound. This is fact, not a story, it has been witnessed and recorded many times. How was this done? Almost certainly I feel at the molecular level, the sudden burst of high energy disrupting the molecules of the glass. Sound can certainly destroy.

We are told that all of manifested creation is organised and governed by one 'root' sound that permeates the entire universe and all that is within it. All of the energy of the universe is created from that one root sound and it is in a continual state of transformation. At each succeeding moment the manifested universe continues to be created anew in response to the continuous root sound and this is the way that the manifested universe evolves from the unmanifested. All of manifested creation is in constant motion and the energy involved is never depleted. Everything that has become visible here on Earth has undergone a sort of contraction into visible form; into a liquid, a solid or a semi-solid. It is as if it were crystallised and it then acts in a way that is governed by the laws of form. The Law of Form as we know it dates from the time of Pythagorus in 580-540 BC. It has of course existed forever but it was first formulated by that great Initiate.

The five solids that Pythagorus described were used by Plato in his teachings in 375 BC and for this reason are called the Platonic Solids. They are the four sided tetrahedron which we know as the pyramid, the six sided hexahedron known as the cube, the octahedron which has eight sides, the twelve sided dodecahedron and the twenty sided icosahedron. Everything on Earth incorporates one or other of these structures. The structure is not always visible to the eye but the formulation or basis can be seen. The forms are present also in energy patterns and are symbolised in that branch of mathematics called geometry. The mathematical order is there in all things and symbolised in mathematics which shows us that everything is interrelated and that intercommunication between everything is possible. This is the basis of Sacred Geometry where the laws apply not only to solids but also to angles and numbers. All this has bearing on sound and understanding. In man, for example, the angle of the female larynx is 120 degrees. This allows the woman to be more intuitive. Women who are particularly sensitive have an angle wider than 120 degrees while the more masculine woman has the angle of the larynx less than 120 degrees, approaching 90 degrees which is the angle of the male larynx.

So the angle determines the sound, or does the sound determine the angle of the larynx?

Sound determines form, and this is nowhere seen more clearly than in the work of Dr Hans Jenny who observed and photographed the effects of sound on matter. He showed that if the spore powder of the Club Moss is spread evenly over a diaphragm and the diaphragm is vibrated by sound waves produced vocally or by an instrument, a galaxy of little piles of powder is formed. Each pile rotates on its own axis and also rotates as a single body rather like our own solar system. Patterns are formed which become more and more elaborate as the pitch of the acoustic tone rises. Apparent chaos is resolved into order. Similarly when liquids are made to vibrate in a similar way, very unusual patterns develop, above all a cellular pattern, not unlike those that are found in the natural world. When the materials and frequencies of sound are changed, beautiful structured patterns emerge; hexagonal and regular overlapping arrangements in the form of honeycomb, network and lattices. Sometimes the texture of the material undergoes a marked change so that once the vibration has ceased we have a different substance, a different type of matter.

This branch of science is called cymatics, the study of the effect of sound upon inorganic matter, the proof that sound is able to create and change form.

Substance is the state in the universe which is similar to a condition in solution just before precipitation. Matter is the precipitate. In the Cosmos, sound moving in orderly sequence causes substance to precipitate and it becomes matter, becomes pattern, becomes the universe as we know it.

Einstein regarded the underlying field out of which matter was precipitated as the ultimate physical entity ... a continuous medium which is present everywhere in space. He saw particles or forms as local condensations of the field in areas where the field is very intense. He saw no place for matter as a separate reality and felt that the field was the only reality. We do not know whether Einstein considered this quantum field as a field of cosmic sound.

Once the substance has been precipitated, what then? Does sound have any further bearing on the form? Let us look from the angle of the Dimensions and endeavour to see the effect of sound on matter which is now in place.

In music when a single note is produced this is called the Fundamental. Other notes also sound and these are in mathematical relationship to the first note. They are the harmonies or overtones. The first harmonic which is sounded vibrates twice as fast as the first note, the second three times as fast, the third four times as fast and so on. It is possible to set in resonance and entrainment frequencies which may be lower or higher than our first sound; sound which we normally cannot hear, such as the deep sound of the Earth Note can become audible. Through this principle of correspondence we are able to use harmonically related sounds to influence the atomic structure of crystals or plant and animal structure.

The principle of resonance is used in industry to convert

sound into light. Different crystals can resonate and amplify different harmonics. The quartz crystal is a good example. The quartz crystal is an oscillator. It can be cut to a specific configuration and tuned by pressure. In this way it produces sound which is subsonic and which in turn produces luminescence. Sound then will produce light.

Peter Tomkins and Christopher Bird state that plant life flourishes when certain music or certain tones are played. Seeds germinate more quickly and sprout faster. More crops are produced when continuous tones of a certain pitch are played. Conversely, random noise and certain notes can retard the growth of plants and even kill them.

Dorothy Retaliak subjected plants to different types of music. She found that when Indian Sitar music was played the plants leant towards the source of the sound. Similarly with Western classical music. The plants remained indifferent to County and Western music and to modern composers such as Schoenberg. But if percussive music such as the steel drum music was played and in particular Hard Rock music the plants leaned as far away as they could. One could hardly blame them!

Shakespeare in *King Henry VIII*, writes:

> Orpheus with his lute made trees
> And the mountain tops that freeze
> Bow themselves when he did sing:
> To his music plants and flowers
> Ever sprung; as sun and showers
> There had made a lasting spring.

Dorothy Retaliak was not the first to observe the phenomenon.

Dolphins and whales are particularly sensitive to sound.

Their hearing is very acute and extends far beyond the human frequency range. Sound travels four times as fast in water as in air. Many members of the whale family (cetacean) do their hunting by sonar or echo soundings. The dolphin sends out sonic or supersonic clicks in bursts of up to 800/second. The sonic information seems to be received by the forehead, which in the dolphin and more particularly in the sperm whale acts as an echo-locating organ, giving directional information. It can then tell the distance, shape, size and species of other animals and fish. The echo is heard with the pitch change of a Doppler effect. The pitch rises as the object draws nearer and falls as animal moves away. The distances are perceived as different rhythmic intervals.

The humpback whale produces musical sounds. The song of the whale in the Atlantic Ocean is different from that of whales living in the Pacific, although both groups of whales have phrases in common. The humpback whales sing a different song each year and the same song extends over distances hundreds of miles apart.

Sound also features at a high level of importance in land animals, in communication between animals of the same species and between differing species for example animals and man. This is speech.

Speech facilitates communication and cognitive activity but may also have had unanticipated effects in the human being. Some neurophysiologists have hypothesised that vocal vibration associated with human use of language caused a kind of cleansing of the cerebrospinal fluid. It has been observed that vibrations may precipitate and concentrate small molecules in spinal fluid, which bathes and continuously purifies the brain. Our ancestors may have, consciously or unconsciously, discovered that vocal sound cleared the chemical cobwebs out of their heads. This practice may have affected the evolution of our present-day thin skull and our proclivity for language. A self regulated process as simple as singing might well have positive adaptive advantages if it also made the removal of chemical waste from the brain more effective.

Vibrations of the human skull as produced by loud singing or vocalisation exert a massaging effect on the brain and facilitate the removal of metabolic products from the brain into the cerebrospinal fluid. The Neanderthals had a brain fifteen per cent larger than we have, yet they did not survive in competition with modern humans. Their brains were more polluted, because their massive skulls did not vibrate and therefore the brain was not sufficiently cleaned. In the evolution of the modern humans the thinning of the cranial bones was important. Changes in diet refined and narrowed the jaw and modified the muscles of the face and throat, facilitating the development of articulation. Only in human has the soft palate 'timed its descent to coincide with the acquisition of language' (K F Tindrak and H Tindrak). Speech facilitates communication and cognitive ability. This was an important step forward.

We probably know more about the effects of sound on the human body than we do about the effect of sound on other animals, although most of our knowledge and understanding is applicable to the animal form in general.

Cells within the body are constantly moving and the movement causes friction and creates sound, in the form of a single note. We could say that tunes are to be found in body chemistry! Amino acids for example are made up of atoms;

basic elementary particles which when grouped together in compound form produce frequencies of sound which form a melody. In a similar way, each organ has its own group of sounds, its own melody, its own song. In very truth the heart sings and the whole body itself can be a symphony.

Composers of music can reflect their own bodily balance in their work by choosing intuitively the tunes within them which are connected to their own rhythm and produced by their cells. Their music then may reflect their own health or illness. We tend perhaps to understand this in terms of mental health but it is also equally true of the health of the physical organs of the body. Perhaps even more so. It is said that some of the music that J S Bach wrote is so close to the sound of the digestive tract that he may had had trouble in this area.

Sound influences life patterns, not only the physical state but mental and emotional patterns. Live sound contains harmonics and overtones but recorded sound does not do this and those people who do not experience live sound may be unable to bring in harmony at the cell level.

The great collective movements of the human soul, says Cyril Scott, have always been anticipated by innovations in music. Handel's Oratorios acted as a brake on the licentious tendencies of eighteenth century England. The music of Chopin awakened a new desire for culture. That of Schuman and Mendelssohn preceded a time of social change, which led to the abolition of child labour and slavery in the West.

The type of music played forms society. It does not reflect society but it anticipates the way society will become. A great deal of the unrest that we are experiencing now has following the introduction of Jazz. Some, by no means all, feel the rhythms of Jazz disintegrate the existing order. Further disintegration of society could be associated with heavy beat music, particularly when performed with strobe lighting.

Sound enters the body through the ear and vibrates in the eardrum. Bone is a prime conductor of sound and the energy is transmitted through a chain of tiny bones to the inner ear. Sound is now a physical vibration. These vibrations in turn reach the cochlea, which is a snail shell shaped organ lying in the area behind the eye. The cochlea is fluid filled and through its coiled lengths are delicate hair-like structures. These are moved by the sound vibrations and are essential to hearing. They are easily destroyed by loud sound. Once destroyed they do not reform and the individual becomes deaf.

Auditory pathways enter the brain through the Medulla Oblongata where the sensory data is 'sifted' by a system known as the Reticular Activating System before it proceeds via the Thalamus to the Auditory area of the Cerebral Cortex. The sifting alerts or sedates the neocortex and by this means affects bodily function. Sound, which comforts and soothes by its rhythm, melody or harmony is thought to reduce stress levels. It lowers the rates of respiration and heart contraction.

An interesting study was made of premature babies. Half of a group of babies were placed in an area where the Brahms Lullaby was played for some hours each day quietly on a loop tape. The other half of the group was kept in a room without music. The 'Brahms' babies were more relaxed, cried less, put on weight and were able to leave hospital a week earlier than the control group.

Resonance is the basis of all sound therapy. It is the basic vibratory rate of an object. If we know the correct resonant frequency of a healthy part of the body, we can project that frequency into the part that is diseased and return it to the normal frequency of health.

Dr Peter Guy Manners who is a pioneer in the study of Cymantics, says:

> A healthy organ will have its molecules working together in a harmonious relationship with each other and will be all of the same pattern. If different patterns enter the organ the harmonious relationship could be upset. If these frequencies are weak in their vibration they will be overcome by the stronger vibrations of the native ones. If on the other hand the foreign vibrations prove to be the stronger they may establish their disharmonious pattern in the organ or other tissues and this is what we call disease.
>
> If a treatment contains a harmonic frequency pattern which will reinforce the organ or organs affected, the vibrations of the intruder will be neutralised and the correct pattern for the organ re-established. This should be a curative reaction.

Many of the treatments of today are designed to do this, the majority being based on sound or light, the two primal energies. These are the healing energies of the future.

Dr Alfred Tomatis in France is one of the forerunners of what is now termed Signature Sound. Much of his work involves retraining the ear to listen and in particular to allow his patients to experience the sounds heard before birth in the mother's womb. The ear begins to develop in the second month of pregnancy and is fully developed by mid-pregnancy. The foetus hears a full range of sounds, most of which contain low frequencies. Before birth the ear is filled with fluid and it is in this watery medium that it is able to filter out the lower more discordant levels of sound, the movements of the organs within the mother's body and the gut sounds. Into this comes the voice of the baby's mother, superimposed upon all other sounds. The baby begins to listen. The mother's voice carries the coded message, which is necessary for growth.

What mother does not talk to her baby, sing to her baby? No harsh notes are involved. The voice is gentle, the harmonic frequencies in the higher frequency bands. This is the medium for normal and natural growth. But, if loud noises are heard, the parents perhaps are quarrelling, the child may stop listening or worse still, the organs within the child's body may be affected in development. Much of the normal growth may be retarded and perhaps it is at this time that the seeds of much future illness are sown.

Rather like the bar code at the supermarket, we carry in our makeup a range of sound frequencies which are essentially our own. Like a fingerprint like a signature, this is our own signature sound.

Sharry Edwards is a pioneer in this field. More than twenty years ago during an acoustic test she found that she had extremely acute hearing which was well beyond the normal human range of 20-20,000 cycles per second and that she also had an exceptional voice and can duplicate pure tone with precision. Later she found that the sounds which she was hearing and duplicating could be related to musical notes which were in 'stress' in a person's speaking voice. By stress, it is meant that the notes were missing or out of tune as indeed were the people themselves. Giving people the pure note back that was stressed in their speaking voice changed their brain frequencies and restored their good health.

The study of Bioaccoustics which has resulted from investigation of Signature Sound has become very complex. The effects of sound on the human body are astonishing but the results make perfect sense. Perhaps at last we have been able to find the note, which will restore and reform the glass that has been shattered by the high note of our singer.

14
LIGHT

Light is a vibrational energy co-existent with sound. We could say that while sound produces matter, light is the producer of form and colour, which is part of light, can mould and alter form. The spectrum of light visible and invisible contains many frequencies and these we appreciate as colour. The range of colour that the human eye can see is relatively limited; unless we can open to higher dimensional energies we rarely see more than a glimpse of the higher dimensional colours.

Animals and in particular birds and insects see different colours from ourselves and many of them can see colour bands well outside the human range. Colour vision is not universal among animals. Primates, including man, see three primary colours, red, green and blue, so gorillas and baboons see the world as we see it. Frogs also respond to similar colours but because their brains are not as specialised as ours they cannot interpret the colour as we might do. Any reaction is an automatic movement. In the face of danger, for example, a frog will leap for the nearest patch of blue:

usually water but it could equally be a blue garment or a patch of blue paint.

Some fish see five colours but the creatures that can see most colour are birds. They have a filter mechanism and can discern more hues than we can. Within the eye a bird has cones and filters adapted to its needs but the sensitivity to red is paramount. Red flowers are pollinated by humming birds, red berries and fruits are used by plants to attract birds and to facilitate seed dispersal. Underwater animals and fish in clear water show more sensitivity to blue light and here red pigment is replaced by blue pigment. But in murky waters where fish like the piranha live, all but the red end of the spectrum is absorbed by the decaying vegetation. The eyes of that particular fish are adapted to see red, with horrid consequences to its victims!

Although we do not, as humans, perceive ultraviolet light as a colour, the retina of our eyes is sensitive to it and the eye filters it out before any damage can be done. Other creatures, particularly insects, are able to see the ultraviolet and to use it in their search for food. Some blue and green flowers have evolved an ultraviolet component to attract bees. Some flowers have ultraviolet marks along the petals to guide the bees to the nectar making sure that in doing so they brush alongside the stamens transferring the pollen to another flower on their next visit to the area.

In the classical past, Pythagoras, Plato, Aristotle and Pliny considered the nature of colour and many of their views were held by great painters such as Leonardo da Vinci. Leonardo wrote,

> The first of all simple colours is white, though philosophers will not acknowledge either black or

white to be colours; because the first is the cause, or the receiver of colours, and the other totally deprived of them. White and black are doorways to spectrums – white contains all colours in our spectrum, black goes into the spectrum. But as painters cannot do without either, we shall place them among the others; and according to this order of things, white will be the first, yellow the second, green the third, blue the fourth, red the fifth and black the sixth. We shall set down white as the representative of light. White light is all encompassing without which no colour can be seen; green for the earth; blue for water; yellow for air; red for fire and black for total darkness – multi-dimensional or spatial.

He did not however attempt to organise colours any further and it was left to Sir Isaac Newton in 1660 to reveal that when white light was passed through a prism all the colours of the rainbow sprang into being. Nothing could have been more exciting than Newton's experiment. His findings revolutionised human thought on light and set into train all the subsequent work in this area. A century later, primary colours of red, yellow and blue were described by J C Le Blon and the Colour Circle described by Morris Harris. His work and that of the many investigators who followed him were mainly concerned with the primary and secondary colours and their use in painting and it was not until later that the nature of colour came under investigation. Much of this understanding came from the work of Johann Wolfgang von Goethe, whom we know mainly as poet and dramatist but who was also an eminent scientist. It was Goethe who first noted that all colours came from black, moving from darkness into light, and Goethe who was deeply connected with its real nature. It was Goethe also who led Rudolf Steiner to experience colour.

We must be able to have colour experience or we cannot grasp what the world of colour is about. We must in some way understand the effects of colour on the world that we live in, understanding that colour is energy and that the different colours are different levels of energy.

In man the major route of entry of visible light into the body is through the eyes. Here the rods and cones transform the physical stimulus of light into neurosensory impulses by photochemical reactions. The resulting electrical excitation runs along two different routes, one stimulating the visual area of the cortex of the brain and the other leading to the hypothalamus. Thus the optic tract conveys the visual picture to the visual cortex enabling us to see and interpret what we have seen, and the second pathway to the thalamus energises our vital functions.

Earlier in this century various investigators had found nerve fibres in the human body which were not present in the optic tract but which appeared to connect the eye to the region of the hypothalamus. Although these findings confirmed previous observations they were not accepted. But recent work by Hendrickson (1972), Moore (1973), Hartwig (1972) and others has proved conclusively that a pathway exists from the eyes to the hypothalamus. Earlier in 1935, Frey had noted that the retinopthalamic pathway was stimulated by light immediately after birth, and that this function preceded the stimulation of the optic tract.

Our present understanding is of a nonvisual pathway from the retina, which stimulates the pineal gland. This tiny gland, about the size of a pea, until recently was thought to be an atavistic remnant of the earlier development of man as a species. It had been noted in the past that the gland contained light-sensitive cells but no definite conclusions had been drawn. We now know that far from being an atavistic remnant, the pineal gland is a vital part of the human endocrine system.

The pineal gland is highly active in humans when they are young and its secretion prevents the onset of puberty and the development of sexual function. It effects this by release of a substance called melatonin, the secretion of which follows a regular daily rhythm. It is released in response to darkness, the highest release level being between two and three in the morning. As the pineal gland is an endocrine gland, it secretes directly into the surrounding medium this case into the cerebro-spinal fluid in which it is bathed. From here it affects both the hypothalamic part of the brain and the pituitary body.

The hypothalamus controls vital functions by both neural and endocrine routes. In this way it affects energy balance, fluid balance, heat regulation, activity and sleep, circulation and breathing, growth maturation and reproduction through the autonomic system, and most of the glandular hormonal secretions through the pituitary gland. It is thus the main controller of our life processes.

The visible part of the spectrum of light does of course enter the body by ways other than the eyes. A small amount enters through the skin where the ultraviolet part of the spectrum produces solitrol, a hormone believed to be part of the vitamin D3. This hormone works in conjunction with melatonin to control the body's responses to light and darkness and influences many of the body's regulatory centres as well as the hormonal system.

The higher reaches of light are also open to us, their main route of entry being the chakra system. The colours within white light are vibrational energies, which are fundamental to the health and wellbeing of the human form. The action is at cellular level within the body and although most of the energy reaches the body cells by the eyes we have seen that the whole structure of our being senses colour and colour vibrations have their effect on the body whether they be seen or not. Every cell within us can perceive the energies of colour because this is a wave pattern of energy that has within it a geometric structure. Its clarity affects the vibrancy of cellular reaction and where there is clarity of colour we find that the cellular encoding receives a pure note. Deviancy within cellular structure occurs because there has been interference with the preciseness of colour and deviancy with sound.

We know the colour of the base chakra as red; we also need to know that the vibrancy of this red is dependent upon the note and also that the vibration takes a shape. The vibrational shape of the base chakra is always rounded. This allows for expansion and retraction of the chakra, mainly because it acts like a sphincter muscle and its nature is to allow the kundalini energies to pass through that channel. This can only happen when the base chakra is able to become a perfect sphere. The speed of this colour and of its energy is what we might call a middle note, rather like middle C on the piano. It has a magnetic nature and draws to itself the substance that is needed for life in that form, for it is the base chakra, which holds the note of life within the body.

The base chakra and the crown chakra act as a duality. The base chakra will only allow the crown chakra to function when a specific chemical state has been reached in that area. This is bio-chemical encoding.

The base chakra holds the key and primacy to animal life on Earth. This is to animal life alone and is instinctive. It does not respond to the higher vibrational note in the same way as the higher chakras respond to that note. The base chakra takes its note from the Earth and is therefore the rooting chakra. There are other chakras, which are at lower points within the causal body, which are in fact lying at a lower level than the Earth's surface, and it is important to recognise this.

We see then that the first dimensional chakra of the third dimensional being has the colour red. This is because in third dimensional terms the colour red is that which stimulates electromagnetic attraction and therefore it is the holding force, it holds all things together. Red is a colour, which holds within it not only the seed of life but also the seed of death. It is a colour that must be respected on all dimensions and all levels, for red can stimulate but it can also destroy.

There is no place upon this planet where the natural rock is the vibrant red of the base chakra. There is a reason for this. There are very few cells in the body that need constant stimulation by this vibration. Apart from the cells concerned with the sexual cycle, the ovum and the sperm, there are very few cells that have a molecular make-up that is predominantly spherical as in the base chakra. The spherical shape on Earth is very much linked to form and red vibrates to the spherical structure. If the colour is given in therapy in too large a dose it will overstimulate and cause explosion and implosion within the body systems. We know that the fastest way to raise the temperature of the body is to stimulate it with the colour red. Overstimulate and we are in for big trouble! We know also that alternating red with the colour turquoise, its complementary colour, will mitigate the effect and prevent overstimulation by red.

Turquoise is not a colour of the third dimension. The two prime colours of the third dimension are red and yellow; with a mixture of these we have orange. Orange is the colour of human consciousness and forms a dimensional bridge. Red, yellow and orange are creative within form and the physical body reacts to these colours within its chemical molecular base and within its subatomic structure. When we start to move away from these colours and these vibrational frequencies, we begin to move into multidimensional concepts.

Yellow is the colour which will balance the endocrine system and in so doing this will stimulate the higher glands as well as the lower. It is the colour that will bring balance to the molecular structure of the physical body. It will also bring balance to the chemical structure without interference with any of the systems. This it does through the endocrine system. Yellow also has the ability to stimulate glands, which would appear to be without function after a certain stage within the body. It has a marked effect upon the thymus, the pituitary body and the pineal gland. These glands regulate balance of hormones and growth potential at subatomic and molecular levels. Using pure yellow we are able to bring in these functional areas and bring about a balance which is not possible in any other way.

Green is extremely healing to the body but too much green may overstimulate some part of the system, particularly in the heart chakra. Often we do not realise this. Green is a bridging colour between the higher and lower chakras and this is its function. When we use the yellow, we do not bridge; we attune to the causal body and to the monadic blueprint. There are many people who are not able to attune to the monadic blueprint or even to the causal body because at this stage they attune to the soul level vibration. These people are living to an optimal soul level consciousness. The majority of those in mass consciousness will not respond to yellow in the same way as those who are light workers. Yellow is a colour that is profoundly healing for all those who have reached the stage of conscious wakening.

Conscious awakening means that a person has united the physical with the soul level and is now responding to the vibrational frequency of the monad. The colour of this frequency is gold and the downstepping of the colour gold is a brilliant yellow. Once we get beyond the lower limitations of consciousness, we begin to feel the resonance of this yellow. We find increasingly that people are reaching the monadic level very quickly and then they respond to yellow, but as they pass the monadic level they no longer feel an affinity to that colour. It is as if they have moved through a gateway, a star gateway, and a great deal of confusion results until they discover their own supermolecular structure.

Green blends with the yellow of the monad and also blends with the blue of the higher levels. Our solar system keys in higher vibrational frequencies to the vibration of blue. The tonal quality of the blue gives breadth and depth. It neutralises. All shades of blue have this capacity to neutralise on different vibrational frequencies and all have the capacity to respond to the note of the Earth's vibration and the Earth's dimensional body. We must understand that the Earth is now fourth dimensional and it therefore works through the first, second, third and has the fifth dimension as its ring-pass-not. All the shades of blue can be used to create a balance structure within those dimensions and the balance is taken from the original blueprint of form for the planet. This is why people on every level of consciousness will respond to the colour blue at every level of their being, for blue is the balance point for the planet on which we have incarnated.

We can now start to understand that each person has their own colour ratio and colour body, not a single colour, but one which is multidimensional, and multifrequential. Everyone has one colour which resonates with the emotional and one resonating with the mental. This is a colour chord or colour hue. When the person starts to answer to the vibrations of the higher levels then it is as if something has to die in order for the new to be born. When this happens a higher colour then takes over. So when we look at someone within mass consciousness we will see within their auric field the colours that most resonate around their physical, emotional and mental bodies. As the person becomes more spiritually advanced and moves beyond the level of personal survival, personal need and greed, they then begin to think in terms not of I, but of we, and become conscious that they are now a team member, then the soul level, the soul colour begins to be very noticeable within the aura and within their expression of life. The transformation has begun.

15
COLOUR AND BODY STRUCTURE

As the earth and its inhabitants move into the higher dimensions, the molecular structure of the body is changing. Cellular structure and body chemistry are changing also, and at a very rapid rate. In the previous cycles of time when body form was being evolved, the evolution of form took thousands of years. But now, in the space of tens of years, the change that is taking place in the physical body is as much as that which took place in all the previous cycles, and higher consciousness is still inhabiting the body. This means that at this time there is no such thing as stability within the body. There cannot be.

If there is change going on in the nervous system, the circulatory system and the basic chemistry of cell structure at one and the same time, there is bound to be some change that is faster than another, some systems that are further advanced. This is why the body at this time is manifesting many strange symptoms. Illnesses are causal in origin because of the change that is taking place in the human body from the causal level. The body is changing its blueprint from the soul blueprint to the monadic blueprint and in some cases even higher. It is changing its vibrational frequency.

The illness that we know as ME is a case in point. It is directly related to changes in the system. The people who are prone to develop ME are those who have had certain vibrational patterns in the sequences of past lives. They have highly developed lower mental bodies that are reluctant to change into the higher mental body form. Movement forward for them is extremely difficult because they do not wish to move from the material level. For some of the sufferers there is a fear of failure in this incarnation. Rather than fall they feel safer doing nothing, in no activity at all. None of this is known to them at the materialistic levels where the illness is felt and where they tend to feel weak, exhausted and fearful.

HIV and AIDS and many of the prevalent diseases of our time can only enter into a vibrational frequency when that frequency is beginning to rise above soul level frequency but is still having difficulties in throwing off thousands of years and hundreds of thousands of lifetimes of conditioning in density in third dimensional frequency. These major diseases of our time cannot be treated by conventional medicine of the third dimension nor can they be treated by anyone other than the individual affected. They are diseases that demand responsibility and internal growth and a dedication to the inner voice, to the higher vibrational frequency that is attempting to gain control of the body. Disease and illness is so often the way of the higher frequency knocking at the door and gaining attention. This is truly where illness occurs at all. Illness arises when there is dissociation between the lower body and the higher counterparts; this may be for some people the lower personality and the soul; for others, the soul to the monad to the I AM. Wherever there is illness it is because there is a hanging-on to old outworn baggage that is no longer needed. But there is a tremendous security in worn out baggage at a deeper cellular level. This cannot be changed unless the change is brought about at a cellular level; otherwise the subatomic structure keeps on rebuilding to the original pattern, the original blueprint. The blueprint is changing and we need to allow the super atomic structure to come in and create this change. Change has to be done from within; we have to begin our new search.

This can be helped but those people who are going to help must recognise that they are the instrument only. Colour is possibly the quickest way to help people begin the profound change. The people who have cellular disease need colour baths but first of all we must stimulate the lower body and create as near a balance as possible. We must do this using the colours of the lower chakras. Once this has been done, then it is important to use yellow or gold. Many people respond to sunlight, which is the most healing of the Rays. People need to bathe within the yellow which allows them to create the new patterning within themselves. It will also stimulate new thought processes. It brings in higher mental vibrational frequencies which may be interpreted as crises. It will seem that nothing that used to work is now working for them. People will then start to look for new avenues of approach to life but the lifestyle must change mentally, emotionally and spiritually. It is then that cases of remission will occur.

We can no longer think of a blanket cover for the Earth because there are still those in third dimensional frequency who still have bacterial diseases. We must realise that bacteria themselves are undergoing vibrational change, and because of this, new bacterial strains will develop. They too are upgrading. Bacterial disease will not disappear from the Earth because there are still third dimensional experiences to be gained. But we are moving now into the region of super viruses and beyond. These are light deviations and are at the same level as photon energy. They are known as prions. The prion gives a deviation in the way in which the cell responds to light vibration. The cellular structure of the body is no longer responding to the chemical nature as it did. It is as if there is a malfunction in the light vibration or in the way in which the light vibration is received in from cosmic energy.

People are not all the same and it is a mistaken understanding that because we are moving into an age of group consciousness and oneness we will lose our individual identity. This will not be so. As we move into oneness we become more identifiable; we are multidimensional and have multidimensional frequencies. It is the balancing of these frequencies that gives us our Note, a note both of sound and colour individual to ourselves. Every individual has a colour chord which his uniquely his/her own.

Because people are not all the same they will react to colour from outside in different ways although the ways will have some similarity, and we must not expect that all the people that we treat will respond in the same way. They are at different stages of dimensional development, each one uniquely individual and individually unique.

16
VALIDATION OF THE SELF

There are very few human beings who feel that they are wonderful, who feel that if they are totally exposed to everything and everyone, that would be all right. We shudder at the thought. Even the most confident of us tend to have issues where we feel vulnerable and dread being exposed. So we deceive ourselves and shy away from the judgements of others, protecting the shadows in our lives.

Hard luck on us; for this is a time when all those protected areas are being brought to the surface, when all the hidden secrets will be weighed in the balance. We have only to pick up the paper and read all about it. Sex, of course, mainly, and more sex, for that seems to be the main interest of people today; or so the papers would have us believe. But there is more to it than that. Our planet has been badly out of balance and this is part of its readjustment. Balance cannot take place without revealing areas of imbalance and pockets of nastiness that need to be cleared.

We are all out of balance and we are doing the very best that we can do. We, you, me, are going through our own learning process. We are surfacing our own darker issues, bringing them out into the light and dealing with them as best we can.

One of the ways that we have developed for protection of the dark areas in ourselves is to get our word in first. If I can look across and put the other person off balance, then he may not be able to see that part of me which I am trying to protect. Many people have developed areas of their personality which are critical and judgmental. Sadly the criticism and the judgement is always heaviest in the critic. It takes courage to move beyond this; to look at one's neighbour and to see the best in them, to honour them for what they are. What then about the things that we don't like in other people? Shrug our shoulders and recognise that is none of our business. We do not have to put other people's lives in order. We need only to tend our own world.

Have you noticed that other people seem to mirror our world? They seem to reflect parts of our own character. Perhaps what we notice is that part of the character that we both share, even though it may not show itself in the same way.

So what is validation? It has many meanings, perhaps because it is often used as a legal term: but in this case it means to recognise or confirm, to honour oneself or others. It means loving ourselves and those around us in a positive and meaningful way. In loving ourself we find that we automatically love other people. We don't necessarily need to like them in order to love them.

The fox, in the children's book, *The Little Prince*, put it in another way:

'And now here is my secret …A very simple secret…It is

only with the Heart that one can see rightly. What is essential is invisible to the eye.'

All the superficial things that we see and judge in other people and in ourselves have no reality – not really.

One of the saddest things about our modern interpretation of love is that we seem to have devalued the word. It has come to be associated with sexual practice, with desire. Yes, there may be love in this but often there is not. It is used for casual greeting: 'mm-mmm, Love you …', and the big sloppy kiss. There is little love in that! And a lot of spit. Love has almost become a negative emotion.

Loving another is not being sentimental. Loving someone is honouring that person as beautiful, even if they are different from you. Even if their beliefs are different. It is in honouring the other and recognising that they have a right to the space that they occupy and if that space is not in harmony with you then you do not need to share that same space, there is space for all in the earth, even though some spaces are rather too hot or cold for comfort. There is space for everyone to have their point of view; being able to walk away if necessary, knowing that you and they have different paths. This is validation in its truest sense. Everyone has their own fears, their own issues that they have come into this world to work through. For those people that you love and honour, those people that you are happy to be with, your honouring of them can be the very thing that helps them to find their purpose, their way, their own answers. It is not for us to interfere.

It is time, that, as human beings, we started to *be*, rather than to *do*. Being means being in truth and harmony with our own light, and only when we can do this can we rightly call ourselves a human being. Doing is so often a means of masking discomfort, a way of not needing to look too closely at our own motives, at the issues that are presenting themselves to us. It is so much easier to *do* because the world justifies *doing*. Isn't it very hard just to *be*? And I am certainly not the best person to tell you how to do it. I can only relay what I have been told and tell you that I have tried my best to follow the guidelines.

One of the most difficult things is just to sit. No expectations. Just sit. If the bell rings or if we hear something, we hear it; if we see something, we see it. But if we don't get involved, we just sit. It's a good practice in Being, for as we practise this we will start to be aware of all the issues in our life that makes us a Doing rather than a Being person. They start to crowd in in physical ways: the chair is uncomfortable, we are gagging for a cup of tea. It must be rather like giving up smoking, which thankfully was not a problem for me because I gave up smoking when Woodbines went up from five for twopence. Then the emotions come in: 'Oh why didn't I go and see so-and-so before she died' – things like that; and finally the thoughts: 'What's the use of all this sitting anyhow. It would be better to so something more sensible'. We must try not to react, to get involved with all the mind talk.

This is practice in Being and as we practise we become aware of all the issues within our lives that attempt to stop or waylay us from being our true selves. It pays off in many ways. You will be amazed how comfortable it begins to feel, sitting quietly in other people's company. So it's worth practising. Each time you look at another and you feel criticism coming into your mind, ask yourself, 'Why do I seem to feel uncomfortable?' 'What do I fear?', 'Where is the threat to me?' It is amazing the answers that come into your mind. The more we do this, we start to discover aspects of ourselves that we didn't even know existed: aspects that need loving and only we can love them, aspects that need accepting and only we can do this. This is being true to ourselves. Remember what that silly old man, Polonius, in Shakespeare's Hamlet said to his son,

> This above all: to thine own self be true
> And it must follow, as the night the day,
> Thou canst not then be false to any man.

Not such a silly old man after all.

Many individuals believe that they are totally honest. But we are not taught to be honest, not as children. We are taught to do what our parents want us to do, what our teachers want us to do. We are taught to fit in with society and more often than not we are taught to be dishonest.

We are taught what is acceptable to feel, what is acceptable to do, what is acceptable to be. And we are taught in such a way that it is never questioned. This is no-one's fault. It has been a very necessary part of becoming an individual and it enabled consciousness to develop.

We must find our own way of switching off, justifying being alive, getting out of the flow of discordant energy that is Doing. We can help each other in many ways but not in this; walking the dog perhaps, or just idly sitting in natural surroundings, most of the without thought. When we first start to practise Beingness we must do it in a way that is acceptable to the people around us.

Nine-tenths of everything we do is not necessary, although

we may feel it necessary. Nearly always the things that we do are because of social expectations. And that's fine. But is the expectation valid? Does it make the world a better place? It seems to me that if we are relaxed and loving to those around us we make the place we're in a better world to be.

If we are tired and fraught with stress because of the pressures of daily life, is that a better place? Picking an argument because we are tired, kicking the cat because it's in the way, feeling annoyed because someone has just entered our space: this is not making the world a better place. Making the world a better place is when you truly come from within yourself, and don't spend your time telling yourself how foolish you are, apologising, feeling guilty and in general putting yourself down.

We don't have to do and be it all. This is a way that we can validate other people. I used to think that to ask for help spells weakness, but I don't think that any more. Perhaps because I am getting older, getting less capable of doing things for myself, I have begun to ask for help. And the results have been wonderful. I have begun openly and genuinely to admire the way other people do the things that I am not good at. From experience, I know how soul-warming it is to be admired. We both feel good. This again is validation.

Think about how good you feel when someone asks for your help and you can give it. We feel good, don't we. So always wherever possible validate those around you. We don't come together in groups by accident. Family, village, town, country, whatever, groups. It isn't by accident. We come because each one of us has something to contribute to the others and that something is just as valid as someone else's something. From being very tiny in our culture, in the society that we live in, so many little lights are screened out. Most certainly, as soon as those little children go to school, because education is an area where learning and knowledge and love for others is not taught. The individual is not valued for himself, only in terms of the brain, the mind and what he does. Those who can do according to the system shine like little stars, one or two out of every class shine. Five or six glimmer. And the rest? They have no feeling of worth, they are not shining, they are learning either to hide behind the desk to avoid notice or to shine in quite another way by being an utter nuisance.

We have all been in this situation; our parents were in this situation too, and their parents and theirs before them. This is the way that it has always been. But we have an opportunity for change now by reaching out one to the other. If it were not for you, I could not bring the message that I need to bring. I need you. Each one of you, of us needs those around us and what perhaps we don't realise, they need you too. They need you whether you are doing or being because it isn't the doing or being that counts, it's you.

No one of us is better than the other. There are always people who will not like what we are doing, what we are saying but there is no need to be other than we are. And if you criticise, remember that there are always going to be people like that who will feel uneasy with what they cannot understand.

Are we happy with all this? Do we have that feeling of at-one-ness with ourselves, at peace? Can we look around us with joy, feeling this is where I would choose to be, this is great. Listen to your heart. This is your measuring stick.

When we come from that place within us that feels the

world is good, then the light shines out of us. But when we feel fear in all its thousand and one forms, when we start to feel inadequate, then there is something that is not flowing for us in our life, that does not bring us peace, that is not feeling good. And this need not be. Our expression into the world can be what we love doing and this is when doing and being become one.

One of the reasons that so many individuals have such problems with health is because they are doing things which do not bring them happiness. There are thousands of ways of expressing our talents, our skills and our uniqueness and this is why we have come into this world. It doesn't make any difference what it is that we enjoy or what it is that brings a warm glow to us, the world needs us and that we have come to give.

What, then, can we give to the world? We can bring peace and harmony. We may be the sort of person who needs a lot of rest and who needs quiet and tranquillity in our life, not the hustle and bustle of everyday. This is a busy doing world and we could be the oasis of peace that many people need.

Other people might like activity, some organise, some are good at figures and books and accountancy. All sorts of people, all types of skills and there is room and a slot for everyone.

If we do what we love to do it brings us abundant energy. Quite startlingly so. So let us try to find out what we are best at doing and do it. What brings us most joy.

It's a very good place to start, and one must be totally honest with oneself. Every time that we are honest and true to ourselves, our light grows a little brighter and it attracts even more light. But if we are not honest, that light dims because we have cut ourselves off from our source. Our source is abundant, available to all. We should ask ourselves, what is abundance for me? We need to find the answer. And when we do find it, we must hold on to it for this is our gift to the rest of humanity. This is our expression of life.

Think about it.

17
On Oneness

I was one of many children and for a large part of my life lived in an old farmhouse on the outskirts of Huddersfield. Not that we were farmers: my father was a manufacturer, and my mother, well, she was just a lovely lady. They were superb parents and we lived a happy uninhibited life, wandering in the woods and fields and learning by experience and through our parents' teachings all about the natural world around us. So, now, although computers are a no-go area for me, I can tell you the ways of sticklebacks, I can find you a caddis fly grub, the nest of the chiffchaff is no mystery to me, and the song of the lark… ah, there is beauty!

Primroses, cowslips, daisy chains… it seemed like everlasting summer.

So, why am I rabbiting on about this? Well the reason is twofold. Firstly, I would like to say a word or two about hens and then talk about relationships – about oneness with nature.

Hens first. Sometimes I feel like a hen, clucking rather aimlessly here and there. More too now than before. To prevent the straying of our hens, we used to clip the feathers of their wings — not much — just so that they couldn't fly easily. It grounded them. I too have had my wings cut; rather cruelly one-sided and I feel like the hens, it has altered my way of life. Unlike the hens, I don't sit about all day but it has altered the inside of me, it has opened up new lines of thought and what is perhaps more important, it has grounded me too, but in another way. I feel closer to nature, closer to the earth — back in some ways to childhood. Yes, I know, you could call it second childhood, perhaps it is, but this time I have a deeper and more profound understanding.

So, life goes on. I'm happy. I see things with new eyes — the weather, the garden, people, plants, animals, birds. I see a oneness running through everything. I live in a smaller house now. A one-up, one-down. Very tiny and only enough room for one. But I have a garden and it would seem that all the birds in Yorkshire come to visit me. Not for myself, but for the food. Not only birds, but slugs and snails, and many smaller creatures. I take the snails for holidays to the nearby woods. I also teach them to fly — over the wall into the next field. There are moles and squirrels too. One of my squirrels eats worms. I saw him, or her, tugging at one after the rain and then swallowing the wriggling mass whole. I had understood that squirrels were vegetarians. I have a squirrel-proof nutfeeder. The squirrels empty it daily, throwing the nuts to the little birds waiting below. There are hundreds of birds in my little garden. From time to time it is invaded by rooks. The rooks post a sentry who caws loudly when I put food out. 'Dinner-time, dinner-time!' it caws. And from every corner of the compass they fly in. Rooks are strange birds, very shy. I have two very old rooks, both with misshapen beaks. They wait until the others have flown back to the fields, and then one leaps on the top of the nut feeder and jumps up and down, up and down. Down fall the little bits of nuts. He and his friend gobble them up. Then he moves to the wall where the wood mice live, and looking carefully over his shoulder to make sure that he is not seen, he tidies up the remains of the wood mouse breakfast.

There are hundreds more birds – all the great tits in Britain, I would say. Great tits are big on procedure – the thicker the black stripe on your breast, the more important you are. Rather like an array of medals. And they make sure that everyone knows it. Only when they have finished eating may the lower orders eat. The lower orders are blue tits, chaffinches, sparrows and any small bird that you can think of.

In midafternoon the greenfinches fly in – in formation; noisy, quarrelsome and full of greed.

You would have thought after this, there wouldn't be a crumb left. Not so. Like the Spanish, most birds have a siesta, a sort of no-go time when it is understood that nature sleeps. Now it is quiet, the little shy creatures move gently in, and rather like domestic staff, begin to clear away the remains of the feast. They post sentries, so that if a cat or hawk is seen, the garden echoes with cries of concern.

When I was working, I never used to notice any of this, but now that my wings are clipped a whole new world has opened up for me and I am beginning at last to understand the world of oneness in which we all live.

And what a world! Language for instance. I understand now most of the bird-calls and they I hope, understand me. Not that language is limited to sound; movements, particularly ritualistic movements, play their part. Movement of the hands, the shoulders, the eyes. And the thoughts! Animals, particularly dogs, cats and horses can both transmit by thought and read the thoughts of others. Most of cat language is thought language. I have only to think, 'It's time for Merlin's pill', to see Merlin, my cat, disappearing out of the door, when a moment earlier he had been fast asleep in the sun.

The cats themselves have tried to teach me their spoken talk.

So far, I know:

'Look out, you're going to tread on me!'

'I have a mouse. It's alive!' We all jump out of bed at this and I have to get there first – to save the mouse.

'I have a mouse, it's dead', a slightly different call. Nobody bothers to move.

'I have no intention of eating that!' A look of disgust and the back is turned on the food.

And many other phrases. It's rather like going to some foreign land not knowing a word of the language. All these strange noises must mean something – but what? – and those hand movements, nods and contortions. But wait – after about a month one knows the essentials, mostly about food and drink and so on. Given a few months, one can get a feel of the shape of the whole and by the end of the year one is thinking and feeling like a native.

And so it is with nature.

Now, let's pause and look at things in a slightly different way. Let us imagine for a moment that we are looking through a microscope at the skin of our forearm. What do we see? Probably very little at first, but as we turn to a higher power, a landscape emerges – what looks like a rather arid landscape of dry caked land and the trunks of many trees. This is of course the outer surface of the skin, a covering of dead cells, the apparent tree trunks are hairs. Turn the high power up further; we are now beneath the outer layers. Here we have live cells, different shapes, with a nucleus, a nucleoii, plasma – the lot! We can see other things as well, numerous pipes, some twisted into spirals, the sweat glands; others carrying blood and nutrients. There are ropelike structures, the nerves and various types of nerve endings.

Let us stop for a moment at this level and consider the individual cells.

I cannot tell you how many cells there are in the average human body. Millions upon millions. More than the whole human race together perhaps. And with the exception of the outer cells of the skin, they are all of them alive. Alive and sentient. Each cell can give and receive energies, the energies of light and sound, of heat. Cells wherever they are, can receive and transmit information. How on earth do they do that? How for example do the cells of the liver tell the cells of the rest of the body that they are out of sorts? Remember the morning after the night before? It was not only the liver that felt ghastly. Remember that feeling of death warmed up! How did the word get round inside us? Well, yes, partly by chemical message through the tissue fluids, but how were these messages sent?

How were they sent? A cell receives a message and transmits it by alteration of its vibrational level. The message from a single body cell is not transmitted by nerves but through the body fluids. There is no direct piping from cell to cell, but each cell is bathed in a medium largely composed of water. Water is a wonderful medium for transmission of information and 99% of the body is composed of water.

No cell is immortal. The body cells that we had at birth, in childhood, even last year's, have long since gone.

The physical body is not a permanent structure with a finite end. It is changing, moving all the time. 99% of the body is open space filled with fluid and is attuned to cosmic intelligence.

There is no part of this finite self that does not totally regenerate within a maximum of twelve months. We remake ourselves with amazing speed. The rate of regeneration depends on the vibratory rate of man on Earth, when the cell structure is totally regenerated, totally replaced within a year. For those of faster vibration, the total cellular structure is replaced within a lunar month, and this means that every cell in the body is replaced within a month.

The patterning that cellular replacement takes is based upon our belief system. If we are following old outworn patterns of thought which take their reality from a perceived length of time or from a perceived state of health, then the new cells will take on the exact state of the old cells. What we believe about ourselves will manifest in ourselves in every conceivable way. If we have cells that are low in energy or that are diseased, the new cells will replace the old in exactly the same pattern unless we can change our patterns of thought. In some ways what we wish to be we become. And so we can change ourselves and become new people by the way we think. We raise or lower our own vibrational level or we do nothing and the level stays the same. Every moment we create the person of the future. Our friends will say, 'What has happened to … she seems to have become a totally new person?' or, 'He's not the man he used to be.'

We can change ourselves, cell by cell for the better or for the worse. This is a supreme example of oneness. From being ill we can become well. We call this a spontaneous recovery and we as doctors cannot explain it.

And for worse? For some years I did a Saturday surgery for a doctor in Huddersfield. Every Saturday, just as the surgery was about to close a very well-looking woman would arrive. A patient. She was always late and always looked the picture of health. But she was convinced that she had cancer. Every Saturday I examined her from tip to toe. She demanded this. From time to time my employer examined her. We sent her for tests, we had X-rays and we sent her to see a consultant physician. None of us found any evidence of disease. This went on for the best part of a year. Then one day when I was doing outpatients at our hospital, one of the nurses came to tell me that this lady had been admitted to the ward. I had seen her on the previous Saturday as usual and as usual she seemed perfectly well. But, again as usual she had, or so she thought, cancer. After outpatients had finished, I went up to the ward, expecting to see the woman I had seen two days before. She was there; she was dead and the abdomen which had looked normal two days before was swollen and lumpy and full of disease. Two days! We are what we believe we are.

This was an extreme example and hard to believe. Two days. But we can think ourselves into almost any condition. Cell then can communicate with cell and thought provides the energy for communication. Within the body only?

Clearly not.

I look at you. You look at me with a smile. You have caught my thought. I look at someone else. They turn away. Heavens, what was I thinking? And so on, and now it becomes even more clever. I look at someone who has their back turned to me and send a thought. And usually that person will turn around in response.

My mother used to say that she had eyes in the back of her head. I believed her implicitly. She wore her hair in a bun and it was there I knew that she kept her second pair of eyes. I felt that they were on stalks rather like a crab's eyes and that she could move them in and out at will. What a way to control!

And I wasn't far wrong. She was aware of all that was going on around. Not through her eyes but through a highly developed awareness of all that was around her. This is something many people have. It is for example the essence of a good family doctor, one of the old sort with a good bedside manner.

Thoughts travel tremendous distances, to the other end of the Earth. Almost instantaneously. Emotions travel. Have you ever been in a crowd when someone has panicked? The panic spreads like wildfire. Suddenly everyone is afraid. Or you have been somewhere where there is complete happiness, complete love. It envelopes you with its sweetness and utter peace. It is as if we were all together in a sort of cloud of knowing.

This is consciousness, the universal consciousness which surrounds us all. We tend to think that consciousness is a personal thing which is confined to the body of a single person. But this is not so. Yes, we have an individual consciousness but we live also in a sea of universal consciousness where all is known, all the past, all the future, everything.

This is the oneness that I have been talking about. As the fish in the sea is surrounded by water, so we ourselves are surrounded by a sea of consciousness, still individuals but also part of the whole as the individual body cell is a part of the whole body.

With the passing years, I see much alteration and most of it is for the good; it is, if you would like it expressed in another way, movement towards the Light. One reason it is not noticed by many people is that the media, television and the press, tend mostly to stress the dark things in life. And being human, we turn to a scandal or a nice juicy murder before reading things like: 'woman of fifty rescues 1,000 snails from certain death'. We seem to prefer the Dark.

But things are changing. We are caring more about our environment, about animal welfare – yes, and about human beings, those who are not so well-off as ourselves, the starving, the hopeless, the war victims. In an odd and rather comical way, the last great war in Europe contributed to this. Evil was revealed as evil and we all saw what Evil can do.

In many ways, Evil is still very active amongst us. We see it everywhere. Our prisons are full, many political systems are corrupt. It is still there but it is now open for all to see, and that, I think, is why there appears to be so much more of it, and why, at last we are seeing it as it is and are prepared to fight it.

The level of vibration in the world is altering. The level is rising – rising towards the Light. And by 'the world' I am referring to our own Planet Earth.

With the Earth is carried all that is within and upon her: the rocks, the plant life, animal life and ourselves. It is like being swept along in a torrent, out to the calm blue sea.

This is not a comfortable transition. Our bodies feel the change and the change is at cell level. So aches and pains and illness of all types, major and minor, are surfacing. Our brains are affected, we tend sometimes to be irrational, we forget, and sometimes we wonder, 'am I going mad?' The answer is 'No.' Emotional illnesses such as ME occur. Physical illnesses are not only more frequent but often more virulent. Even bacteria and viruses are evolving. And we are moving together with everything else, towards the Light.

We cannot stop progress but we have a certain amount of control over what is happening to our bodies. We can change from the cell level upwards by thought, by our patterns of thought. Find moments in the day to allow the higher side of ourselves to move into every part of the body, into our life, the way we live and think. We should practise seeing and visualizing every part of the body in the most perfect health; visualize ourselves as we would wish to be and bring this into our reality. For if we believe that we are inadequate, we become inadequate, we become inactive and our cellular vibrations are reduced, allowing illness and unworthiness to take over the body

So we do this for ourselves but what about other people? We owe it to them to help. Other people have made mistakes, others feel inadequate. By seeing the best in others, seeing their truth worth and telling them so, we bring out the best in them, bring out the beauty in them, affirming what they are strong in, and in this way we lift the vibratory level of their cells.

It is our belief that produces our state of mind and produces chemicals for regeneration and the new birth of cells at their optimal level. Every time that we can say to a person that they are enough, and say it in truth, say that they are just where they should be, that their life has meaning for us and that we thank them for being, we are in essence giving them a boost of regrowth chemical. This is the stuff of miracles, it is the type of chemistry that can shrink tumours, that can bring about cellular regrowth in a balanced harmonious way, that can eradicate disease from within the body. For when a person feels total love within and around them there is no disease in the body.

This is so vitally important that it bears repeating. Every time that a positive thought is felt about ourselves or about another, it produces a stimulation of the chemicals which produce new life in its most positive form. Any defect, any inadequacies, are irrelevant; they only exist for as long as the cellular expression exists, unless they are remanifested into reality. For cellular changes, the total rebirth of the whole physical body happens even with the slowest vibrations, yearly. Most people vibrate at a higher rate. Seventy per cent of humanity at this time change all of their cells in as little as seven months, thirty per cent within three months and two per cent of humanity changes its cellular expression within one month.

No matter how the physical condition is disabled, there is no failure. If a person has disease within them to such an extent that they cannot stop the disease process then it is possible that the physical body will have to die. Disease is the reflection of the belief pattern that we have had over many thousands of years, life after life, until the disease process becomes manifest. Death is not a failure but rather is it another chance to remake and remodel ourselves in the next life on a higher level.

As we start to practise different beliefs about ourselves, possibly the easiest way to practise it is through meditation, when we are in touch with the higher self. As we do this we have the opportunity to change at the cellular level totally. But we must also make a conscious effort to validate others, helping each other to bring about cellular change and transformation.

I have thought a lot about God recently; in fact I have wondered about Him all my life. No longer do I feel that He is the God of the Old Testament, an old man with a long beard and a tendency to punish when we most deserve it. Rather, I think that He is one with the birds and the bees and the flowers and the trees, and man if we would but let Him, the Supreme Energy that holds us all together and makes us into a oneness. We are part of God and God is in a sense within each one of us, within the squirrel, within the greenfinch, within all that is good and beautiful but also there within the hell-holes of suffering and unhappiness. For this reason I would like to end this chapter with the meditation which for a long time now has epitomised my understanding of God:

> 'I am the Oneness, the Whole. The indivisible Ether of all that is. I am in you and all people. I radiate from you. The cosmic vibration of my essence draws those to you who seek My Presence. I speak through You and reach out to touch the hearts of all that you encounter. I am Light. I am Love. I am all things Good. I am Spirit. I am matter. I am Life. I am Knowledge. I am Wisdom. I am Understanding. Nothing can eradicate My Light. I am in the highest and lowest. The deep and the shallow. The night and the day. In all Nations

and in all Galaxies. I surround you and dwell within you. I am one with You. My oneness unites you with the oneness that I express in others.

…Never separate…Never different…Never isolated…Never superior nor inferior. I simply am. There is nothing that you cannot do through Me. I hear all. I see all. I understand all. My substance is Joy, Love and abundance. What is true of me is also true of You. I am constant, steadfast and true, yet my essence is freeflowing and creative. I am You. I am He. I am She. I am plant. I am animal. I am tree. I am all that is. I AM.

18
LOVE, LOVE ALTERS EVERYTHING

Residence upon Earth demands that we make choices and there are truly only two. We can choose to love and the path of love leads to happiness or we can choose to fear and the path of fear leads to imbalance and debility within the physical body. There are truly only those two major choices. Being unhappy does not mean that we have failed, we have not done anything wrong, but unless that part of our energy that needs loving is surfaced, unless it is acknowledged, happiness is a long way off.

Man's urge to love in all forms is intense; all our popular music speaks of the search for love, or its heartaches, its traumas and its joys. We associate love with joy, which is probably why it is so eagerly sought after. We associate it also with peace, with quietness, with harmony and with content. And sometimes with exuberance, for love is at the same time both a public and a personal energy, and this is so often misunderstood. We may think of love as great waves of emotion expressed by thousands of people shouting and sobbing, and yes, there may be great love in this but so often it will be followed by a wave of negativity where hate and blame are apportioned by those who do not understand. Is this truly love? I think not.

To understand love fully we have to accept that it can include great pain. Love itself involves pain and suffering. Love is a feeling energy and does not work alone. It is never detached from life. Love for others means that whilst we may share their joys, we also have to share their sorrows and pains. When someone is in anguish and suffering love does not walk out of the door, it stays and comforts them until the suffering has departed.

Love embraces fear and absorbs it until that also departs. Love walks in to the hell-holes of life where people fight tooth and nail to survive and speaks to those who can hear its voice of caring and of brotherhood. It shines its light in the darkness of evil and never turns its face away.

Love does all these things, and more.

St Thomas à Kempis, the great fourteenth century mystic, echoing the words of St Paul, wrote:

> Love feeleth no burden, it accounteth no labour, it desireth more than it may attain, it complaineth never of impossibility, for it deemeth itself mighty to all things and all things be lawful to it. It is valiant therefore to all things, it fulfileth many things and bringeth them to effect where he that loveth not faileth and lyeth still.
>
> Love waketh; and sleeping, it sleepeth not; love wearied is not weary, and love constrained, it, afraid is not troubled; but as a quick flame and a burning brand, he burneth upwards and passeth safely.

For love is an energy, the highest feeling energy of all. In very truth it is Love that makes the World go round.

In this world all energies are vibrational from the highest to the lowest. At the bottom of the scale are the mechanical energies and as the rate of vibration increases the energy becomes the energy of sound, as we know it, of colour, of electromagnetism, right up to the higher energies of the spirit. And the highest energy of the spirit is Love. Love is the energy of attraction, the great cohesive factor, without which we would not exist; it holds the stars together, it governs the workings of the earth; it unites the atom. It is the mediating energy between the negative and the positive, tending always to the balance. It is the creative energy within us all. Love is everywhere, not only in human and spiritual relationships, but also in gravity, in magnetism, in electricity, in sound, in colour and in healing.

I was profoundly influenced in my early thinking by an American Theosophist called Marie Poultz. Reflecting on the love of the higher beings for man, she talked about the apparent inconsistency of what she called Heavenly Love. She says, discussing the morality of right and wrong:

> My thoughts turned to those who have transcended humanity, for they seemed to condone what the commandments given by some amongst themselves forbid men to do; it seemed even in some cases as if those whom they chose to admit into their ranks earned that privilege by apparent mistakes and wrongdoings.

And as she pondered on the problem, she had a sudden insight into how those above us look upon love. She seemed to see humanity as divided, not as we see it with a horizontal line drawn between those who are ready to enter the Kingdom of Heaven and those who are not, but in an entirely different way; she saw a vertical line dividing the people of this world and the division this time was between those who loved and those who did not love. She saw on the positive side all those people who had ever shown love in any form; and these included not only those who truly loved humanity, but the prostitute who gave love to those who had none, the drunkard who expressed love for himself, and even the miser with his love of money. All these she saw were nearer to the true expression of love than those who did good deeds because it was right or because it was their duty. She went on to say:

> and I saw that many I had condemned were on the side of love, and others whom I had admired were on the other side in spite of their splendid achievements, because of their lack of sympathy and understanding. I believe I have caught a glimpse of the measuring standard of those more than man. And when confronted by the moral problems of daily life, I am humbly learning to ask, 'Is it Love?

Love is involvement with life, for through life and its experience, we learn how to love. People who love are not shut away in ivory towers, for they care for others as much as they care for themselves. It's very easy to love the clean and the knowledgeable, the pleasant easy-going people in this life; it's far more difficult to love the dirty, the uncouth, the smelly and the depraved. But love embraces all people, no matter who they are: it seeks out the goodness in others and nurtures it as it grows. Above all love is silent about that which it does.

One would expect those souls who have learned all about

the higher spiritual energies and who have passed the need to incarnate again on this plane, would dwell on some remote faraway place, directing the fate of man from afar. And there must be those who do this. But the greatest of these, perhaps those who have 'seen God's face', are never far away from us, and the acts of great tenderness and mercy and charity which we see on our Earth, have behind them their energy and their love for all things. They have no names, no form; they do not need them, for these things are of the material world and the lower planes of consciousness. They do not teach any creed or expound any philosophy; they do not need to for love itself has no barriers. It just is.

It was not until recently that I realised that love and fear cannot exist together. Where there is true love, fear goes out of the window. And I thought of the wild animal protecting its young, of the bird leading the predator away from its nest by pretending to be lame. I thought of the soldier braving gunfire to help a wounded comrade. All acts of incredible bravery and love. Those who have given their own lives for their friends.

Were they afraid? I'm sure they were, before and after, but at the time, I think not. I have my father's First World War diaries. Scruffy little notebooks written in smudgy pencil. My father was a sweet gentle man, a truly loving man and he was much bemedalled. The entries read 'crawled out with Cpl. Brook under enemy fire to rescue wounded. Brook killed at my side. Writing to B's wife.' This was the Somme, the killing fields of France.

Nothing can glorify war, nothing; yet it is at times like these that Love may be the true victor.

Real love is a high energy and at these levels fear cannot

exist. And when we have come into this level of love, which we all do from time to time, we find to our surprise and pleasure that we are no longer afraid. And this is wonderful. We don't of course go out and do silly things, deliberately standing in the line of fire. We don't court disaster, but we can and do stand up to situations without fear and we can love and be loved without prejudice. We needn't pretend any more.

How do we find it, this Shangri-La of feeling, this haven of perfect peace? Let us start by being happy. Just by being happy.

I remember a pantomime song long ago at the Grand Theatre in Leeds. It went something like this:

> Today I am so happy, so happy, so happy.
> Today I am so happy, so H-A-P-P-Y.

And so on. It was a lovely song. A great sheet came down from the sky and there were the words. The row of little sunbeams and the Brierly family sang it again and again at full voice.

'Today I am so happy.' We went on singing it and sang it through January and well into February until the happiness song was forbidden. And then when Mother was not listening; we would sing it very very softly.

We tend to think it wrong to be happy. Perhaps this is because we believe that we can fail. We believe that we are not beautiful, that in order for others to love us we must create a role, another person.

The most important thing that we can do is to learn to love ourselves. This is not a selfish act because until we can reclaim our inner balance, until we can reclaim that inner love, we cannot put pure love out into the world. This above all is what the world needs. Not the second class conditional love that is given by the unloved masses.

If we criticise or judge our energy in any way we automatically debase it and this is particularly true of love. And when we wish to use it in the service of others we find that it is of little value. It's as if we reach out to heal others but have not first healed ourselves.

We heal from a wounded persona and we pass on the wound through the healing. Many healers nowadays are wounded healers and their performance, for it is so often a performance, shows this only too well.

We must love ourselves, heal ourselves, and be true to ourselves, aiming back to the joy and the beauty, which were there when we were children. We must release all that is not well; release the need to control our lives; get into the habit of doing what is really comfortable for us and listen to the inner voice of happiness. There is no sin in being happy or loving. No guilt. So spread it around, enjoy it and be abundant.

Do you remember 'Laughter at four, tears before bedtime'? Perhaps you never heard the saying. It was one of the early put-downs to being happy. An early conditioning. And we have been conditioned throughout our lives not to show joy or happiness. It might make other people feel bad. It's a very negative way to live. We must release the negativity and be generous to ourselves.

'It might upset other people'. And so we go to church, solemn faces, hell around the corner, miserable sinners. We go to a funeral, same thing. The dead person has gone to Heaven, dammit, after a long and painful illness. The suffering is ended. Why can't we be glad? And why can't we show it? Who are we sorry for?

Remember Christian in *Pilgrim's Progress*, who finally and after much suffering crossed the river and entered the Gates of the Kingdom? 'And the trumpets sounded for him on the other side!'

Who are we to spoil it for them?

So next time we go to see someone who is ill or dying, instead of the grapes let us take them happiness, let us take them love, let us open our hearts so that energies of love may flow into them. We may be surprised at what happens.

It seems that love is the stuff of miracles if we can allow it to be so. At birth we are innocent and happy, open to the world; but from then onwards we are conditioned by our parents, our teachers, our peers. We learn that unhappiness can be productive. Children often feign unhappiness in order to get their own way. It makes their parent feel guilty or mean and one is tempted to give in to their demands. In a similar way adults often feign illness for the reward that it brings: comfort, attention and, again, a sort of love. It is the way we look at life, which determines our experience. The beliefs that we create shape our thoughts and actions, often in a never-ending circle of unhappiness.

Love, true love, can alter this.

Barry Kaufman, describing how he and his wife transformed their autistic little boy into a highly intelligent youngster by totally surrounding him with love and attention writes:

> When we greet people's discomforts and self incrimination with an attitude of love and acceptance, they tend to relax their guard and begin the process of unearthing the beliefs that have fuelled their

unhappiness. Their struggle becomes a dance. Judgements melt away. They become more self-trusting and self-accepting. They develop a sense of inner peace. They realise that they are not against themselves in spite of self-defeating behaviour; in fact they begin to do the best they can and start acting with the best intentions.

So love can change our lives, the love of one person for another, the love of one person for himself. Have no doubt about that.

Love alters everything.

19
Practise Random Kindness And Senseless Acts Of Beauty

I first met this little saying many years ago and found it full of delight. What a way to live!

And that was long ago.

Recently to my surprise the little phrase surfaced again; 'Practise random kindness'.

And I began to understand that this is what we must do. This is the key to relationships. It is a vital message at this time and many people are waiting to hear it. It is the key which will unlock future development for thousands upon thousands of people.

In the lower dimensions where we live and have our being, people think of themselves as finite. They notice change all around them but they fail to see that change is taking place in the physical body, that the body itself is transmuting. They are not able to access the higher energy that is needed to understand that they are eternal and that this physical self is only a manifestation of the eternal self.

One energy flows through us all; nothing about us is finite; everything is infinite. When we incarnate we lose track of the infinite whole, and the small part that is left, the one per cent bit, is what we regard as the finite self that has a linear time here on earth. This, we believe, is our reality that we feel we cannot live without.

The speed of regeneration of body cells is incredibly fast and we have talked about this elsewhere. Think of it, a new body every twelve months and the major part of this structure is tuned into to Cosmic intelligence, to higher levels of thought. Were this not so, we could not exist! There are many schools of higher thought. They all teach that the perception of our own self-worth is vitally important at this time, and the importance of relationships is crucial so the more each of us can validate each other the more they will help that person to validate himself. Validation means not only recognising a person's true worth, but telling them so. There is no more crucial issue at this time than each individual perception of self-worth. If you are what you believe, high felt worth produces high vibratory energy. If we are living a life which has not led to feelings of high worth we develop a belief of inadequacy within ourselves. And this belief of inadequacy can render us inactive and can reduce our cellular vibrations and allow illness and feelings of unworthiness to take over our bodies.

This is where the 'random acts of kindness' is important. Let us practise validating people, seeing the best in them. Seeing their true worth. This brings out the beauty in them, it affirms what they are strong in, it lifts the vibratory rate of their cells. And we should also do this for ourselves; never be afraid to acknowledge to ourselves our true worth.

There is no act too small if it leads to the validation of another human being. A simple loving act or gesture, an affirmation of the person being enough, being totally where they are meant to be, how they are meant to be, when they are meant to be.

No matter if a person feels that they have made a mistake, or if they feel that they are inadequate. Remind them that their inner self is far from being inadequate, that their higher self is God-like. The higher self does not make mistakes: where they are now is exactly where they are meant to be. Every moment we are creating our new self. If we feel totally at one as we are, then we will create wholeness within ourselves. We shall create our complete being. There will be no accidents. I am whole, I am enough, I am exactly as I am meant to be.

In the doing and in the believing of this we will make the most dramatic changes within our body chemistry. When a person grieves, despairs, feels woefully inadequate, they exude chemicals within the body, which act as poisons to the body. We could call them Death Hormones, for they create chaos. They are scientifically measurable; we are no longer dealing with esoteric belief. We know now that what a person believes affects their chemical constitution, and this in turn totally determines their environment, their world and their perception. When a person smiles, laughs and is happy, that produces life-enhancing hormones, life enhancing chemicals, enabling cellular regeneration of the most positive kind.

It is our belief that produces our state of mind and produces chemicals for cellular regeneration and the new birth of cells at their optimal level. Every time that we can honestly say when we look at another, 'You are beautiful', or 'You are worthy', what you are doing in truth is giving them an injection of positive hormones just as surely as if you were taking a full syringe and injecting its contents. Every time we say to a person that they are enough, that they are where they should be, that you thank and honour them for being there, that their life has meaning for you, you are giving them an injection of regrowth chemical. This is the stuff of miracles; it is the type of chemistry that can shrink tumours, that can bring about cellular regrowth in a balanced harmonious way, that can eradicate disease from within the body. For when a persons feels total love within and around them, there is no disease within the body.

So, let us be nurturers one of the other.

Let me repeat myself. I am sure you will forgive me.

Every time that a positive thought is felt, about oneself or about another, it produces a stimulation of the chemicals which produce new life in its most positive form. Any defects, any inadequacies are irrelevant, they only exist for as long as the cellular expression exists unless they are remanifested into reality. For cellular change, the total rebirth of the whole physical body happens even with the slowest vibration, yearly. Most people vibrate at a higher rate. Seventy per cent of humanity at this time rechange all of their cells in as little as seven months, thirty per cent within three months and two per cent of humanity changes its cellular expression within one month.

No matter how disabling the physical condition may appear to be it is only the reflection of the belief patterns that we have had over many thousands of years. Life after life until the disease of the cell begins to manifest.

As we start to practise different beliefs about ourselves, possibly the easiest way to practise is through meditation and being in touch with the higher self which is constant and loving and self-affirming. As we do this we have the opportunity to change at the cellular level totally. But we must also make a conscious effort to validate others, helping each other to bring about cellular change and transformation. This is possible for us now and clearly within our reach. All that seems to prevent us is a false illusion. We cannot see the truth, which is staring us in the face.

There is no failure in this; if a person does not manage to change their cellular patterning and they have disease within them to such an extent that they are not able to stop the ageing or disease process, then it means that the physical body has to die. This is not a sign of failure. As long as that person has changed their perception, has begun to practise random acts of kindness, as long as the validation of self and others has become part of their process, that is all that matters. It is all that matters because on the multidimensional level, healing is taking place and is ongoing. Whether we are incarnate or not incarnate, all of our thoughts are producing the next form of cellular structure that we will take on in any dimension. So this healing on all dimensions is crucial, there is no failure. Every time that we think a validating thought of self or others, then we have produced within ourselves and others a healing change.

When we are talking to each other the important thing is that we must never lie. The things that we say to each other must always bear a truth. On the deep cellular level only truths are recognised. If we say something to be flattering which we do not believe then it can be magnified by all the negative forces and the person knows at the cellular level that there is no truth there. So rather than validating, it devalues that person, it lessens their self-worth. When we speak it must always come from within, from the inner self.

So:
'Practise random kindness and senseless acts of beauty'.
'And senseless acts of beauty'?
Sensitive perhaps, not senseless. These are, I feel those little acts of love that pass between loving friends – a flower perhaps – a feather – a hug – even tears in the eyes – or laughter.
Yes, laughter!

For I am reliably informed from an impeccable source that laughter is the currency in Heaven.

20
Living In The Fast Lane

'What is this life if, full of care,
We have no time to stand and stare?'

There is a tremendous focus on action in our materialistic Western World. The recent changes that have taken place are truly remarkable when we consider that at the beginning of the last century there was no such thing as the family car, that the use of electricity for lighting and communication was in its infancy. No radio, no television and the computer was a non-existent dream. Everyday things which are now taken for granted did not exist in the early nineteen hundreds, but since then not only the car, the radio, the television, but air travel and planetary exploration are everyday happenings. The computer seems to have taken over our lives; the atom has been split and genetic engineering is well under way.

Human development has speeded up and with this, the development of human consciousness and human values. Human values have changed to the extent that people are almost likened to the machines that they use for convenience. They are no longer seen as energy fields but rather as units on a production line, as robots.

We tend to feel guilty if we take time to look around us, if we stop to admire the view, if we watch the beauty of a sunset and allow that beauty to enter into our very being. There is no time today to feel the silence or to sit and listen to the sounds of nature. In the words of the poet, W H Davies,
> No time to see, when woods we pass,
> Where squirrels hide their nuts in grass:
> No time to see, in broad daylight,
> Streams full of stars, like skies at night;
> No time to turn at Beauty's glance …

No time! And this is life today for the majority of people.

No time! And this is the sad part of our existence here, for these very things are not idle pastimes. They are the way the body is able to rebalance, to reset and to heal itself.

There is a need for all of us who live in this heavily material world to have times of quiet, moments when we can allow our bodies the opportunity to regenerate and for healing to take place in every part of our being. In the physical, emotional and mental levels, through stillness. Only when this occurs is it possible for the Higher Self to make itself felt, to make contact and communion with this extension of its energy that is so immersed in heavier denser vibration. The connection with the Higher Self is vital if humanity is to follow paths which lead to wholeness and healing both for the human race and for the planet itself. When human beings rush around like headless chickens, they create turmoil wherever they go, living through the lower nature which is, by virtue of its kind, selfish and self-orientated. It is defensive; it is separatist, causing friction, impatience, all negative energies. Through lack of thought and caring, it causes the development of those things which not only will destroy the planet but which will destroy incarnation upon the planet.

This has to stop. We must be very aware that even 'Lightworkers' can fall into the trap of filling their lives beyond the capacity that they are capable of enduring. They, in common with all other human beings, have been conditioned to believe that the 'doing' state is the state that brings benefit. So often if there were not the mad rush there would not be the need for the pause. Humans have got into the habit of thinking that if they are busy, if they are doing, they are automatically keying into their purpose. What we need from all of us at this time is a pause. We need to still our energies and to bring them into balance as much as is possible; to bring beauty and peace into our lives at times when we are not active. Each one of us who is able to maintain this state, helps to stabilise the extremely turbulent energies on and around the Earth at this time and which are also within humanity. Because of this turbulence it is very difficult for healing Rays and transformational vibrations to make an impact. We are needed to bring about 'a pregnant pause', a moment of stillness, a time where others can be in touch with everything that for them is beautiful, be it the perfume of flowers, music, the sky at night, or whatever brings that deep inner peace. That is all that is asked at the moment.

We must not run ourselves into exhaustion and it is vital that we should attempt to slow down this fast-moving train. There is a momentum that is causing human consciousness to hurtle in an unguided fashion towards destruction. It is very difficult at the present time for the higher energies to make themselves felt. The distractions of this life are many and they may seem very authentic, they may seem unavoidable, but look to what is truly important, do what is necessary, maybe accept that there is need for realignment of priorities and that the main priority is that what we do, how we do it, where we go, manifests a stillness within us. If we are feeling burdened or overstressed, if we are feeling overtired, then it is a signal that this is a time to be still. One has to respond to the moment and this may make forward planning difficult but it is not impossible. It is in times of stillness that the Higher Self can make contact. It may ask of us very special tasks, those perhaps that bring in the special energies that one can find in a bluebell wood, or a garden, or perhaps listening to certain types of music or looking at paintings, perhaps in the company of others, in stillness and quiet. If all our time is organised and spoken for it is not only very difficult for the Higher Self to ask what it needs of us but also difficult for us to fulfil that need.

One of the reasons that we find ourselves debilitated is because we are too busy. It puts us out of action. The higher energies cannot make contact, they are blocked. Deliberately blocked. At this time many people are being offered distractions that seem very authentic. They are working for others, for their fellow man, all the hours God gives. They are so involved that they're not able to tune in, not because they're unwilling but simply because there is no time to do so, the distraction seems too authentic. How can we know what is required of us? ...When in doubt be still.

Most of the imbalance at this time in the Western World is because our bodies are never given the time to regenerate. There is no time to be ill. Illness is the body's way of telling us that it is out of balance and needs rest. Many of us enlightened beings will allow it to rest for twenty-four hours, perhaps a week or two. But the body may need more, perhaps a year or more. During this time we can allow our Higher Self to guide us and we are allowed to get out of the rat race and let peace and stillness to flow into us and through us into the outer world. John Milton, if you remember, says, 'They also serve who only stand and wait'. And this is so. We stand and wait and listen.

At this present time the Alternative Therapies are very busy training therapists. People to heal other people. One wonders if for some people this is the negation of taking responsibility for themselves. The emphasis is always on healing from the outside, but we know that healing can only take place from within. It would seem that if we have the faith to listen to the inner voice, having the faith to be, as well as the faith to do, and get the two in balance, there would not be the need for all the different therapies. It is the intention to heal or be healed that is important. So often helping others is an escape from truly finding out what we need to sort out in ourselves and it is this search for wholeness that leads us into forms of healing that we try to impose upon others. Literally, so often these healing techniques are imposed.

Healing must come from within both in ourselves and in others. We can help and advise but we cannot force the process. And for ourselves we must remember that we come with our own manual but this manual can only be accessed by being quiet and still and listening. By turning inwards. Some people can do this by quietly pottering, perhaps in painting, growing, cooking, or doing a gentle activity that brings joy. Something that we choose to pursue in a creative manner, that is done in an unhurried way and which allows them to tune in to a higher energy. This brings healing: it also brings people to a point where they are able to look at and reassess their life. There is no need to follow the herd. What is necessary for us is to learn to listen to the inner voice, to listen to what is true for us, find our values and then look at life to find how these values can be expressed.

But, we will say: we have to live, we need to work in order to live. And this is true, but we have entered this world to bring a gift and that gift is a quality that can be expressed through our living. If we remember this and trust our higher self we will not want – work will come our way and we will lack nothing. By sharing and by following what we love to do we can also live, even in a world that is material.

In his Christmas address in 1939, after the outbreak of the Second World War, King George VI said:

> And I said to the man who stood at the gate of the year: 'Give me a light that I may tread safely into the unknown'. And he replied: 'Go out into the darkness and put your hand into the hand of God. That shall be to you better than light and safer than any known way.

I think we should do the same.

Daily Help

On rising, visualise the personality as a ball of light that centres within the chest area; and then rises to the top of the head.

Visualise a connection with the Higher Self made from this ball of light, rather like a stream of energy that plugs into a Higher Energy connection and allows you to turn a switch on to the intuition there.

Plug this in *every morning*.

At lunchtime, once again get in touch with that light, but this time flood all the personality, all the body, with light. See it flowing through the Crown Chakra – through the body – out through the feet; and then going round the aura. The light stretches out through the aura and cleanses it. Whatever negativity we have picked up until now is cleansed out of the aura.

In the evening, visualise a rose-pink light lighting the higher chakras and then giving way to a peach-coloured light.

If you find that your energy is thrown into discord, or something is occurring within your life that is making you panic, that is draining your energy, that is throwing you off centre, again, make a connection that starts at the solar plexus and works up through the higher chakras. Make the connection very strongly. See the chakras flooded with light, within yourself. Keep on making that connection until the negative emotion has passed away.